C000182697

# PROBLEM SOLVING TECHNIQUES THAT REALLY WORK

# PROBLEM SOLVING TECHNIQUES THAT REALLY WORK

MALCOLM BIRD

First published in 1992 by
Judy Piatkus (Publishers) Ltd of
5 Windmill Street, London W1P 1HF



*A catalogue record for this book is available from the British Library*

ISBN 0–7499–1109–3

Edited by Carol Franklin

Set in 11/13 pt Linotron Plantin Light by
Phoenix Photosetting, Chatham, Kent
Printed and bound in Great Britain by
Biddles Ltd, Guildford & King's Lynn

# CONTENTS

# Introduction

According to the *Concise Oxford Dictionary* a problem is a 'doubtful or difficult question or task'.

*Webster's Dictionary* goes a bit further and defines a problem as 'A question raised or to be raised for enquiry, consideration, discussion, decision or solution'.

Business people will, in particular, recognise the terms 'doubtful or difficult' and 'decision or solution', since business problems often involve doubtful facts and figures (or none at all), present a degree of difficulty and invariably require a solution. Achieving the solution requires the taking of a decision.

And that is what this book is all about. It deals with those situations in which a course of action must be decided upon when the information immediately available does not point to the solution. Indeed, it can be argued that if the information available does clearly point to the decision to be taken then no problem exists!

Sadly, this situation is rare and we are often faced with choosing from a number of 'solutions' (including doing nothing at all), with no absolute certainty of the outcome.

The process and techniques described in this book are designed to enable decision-takers to maximise the degree of certainty – even where little or no data are available. No 'magic formula' is offered, however, as none exists! Nor does the book offer an easy way out of problem solving – the degree of success will normally be proportional to the amount of care and effort put in. However, users of the methods described can expect a higher hit rate than would be achieved by the seat-of-the-pants school of decision-making.

So, who can use this book?

Anyone who has to solve problems in their work should find it useful. The book will help you in answering questions as varied as these:

- How many machines do we need?
- Should we build our new factory in location A or location B?
- Will a bonus scheme improve our productivity?

- How can we reduce manufacturing costs without reducing product quality?
- Should we go for export sales?
- Should we take the additional space which the landlord is offering at a 'bargain price'?
- To advertise or not to advertise?

Whatever the problem, the *process* described in this book will apply. One (or more) of the *techniques* is likely to be helpful and readers must exercise some judgement as to which is most appropriate to the particular circumstances they face.

## How can this book be used?

It is hoped that the book will be found digestible enough to read right through to obtain a broad appreciation of the right approach to problems.

When faced with a significant problem the reader can then use the book as a reminder of what must be done and as a source of ideas.

For instance, Part 2 suggests ways and means to collect information and Part 3 shows ways in which analysis can be used to draw sensible conclusions from the information.

Quite frequently, completion of the process thus far will indicate one or more potential solutions to the problem. However, life is not always that kind and there is a chance that even after our best efforts we will still be in trouble.

For example, we may find ourselves in the following situations:

- We may have insufficient time to collect information. With the warehouse on fire there is no time to investigate the market in fire extinguishers!
- We may have some of the relevant data but not all. Some may be unobtainable.
- Much may depend on the unpredictable action of other people.

- We may doubt the accuracy of some of the information collected.

In such circumstances we may need to resort to some gut-feel decision-taking. This, as is explained in the book, is not such a wild and woolly approach as some authorities would have us believe, providing we use our gut-feel in a controlled way. Part 4 provides you with some ways and means to do this.

Part 5 gives guidance on how to enhance the chances of your chosen solution actually working in practice. It is not unknown for the right decision to be taken but for faults in implementation to result in disappointment. Part 5 can be consulted for the necessary steps to be taken *before* putting a decision into effect.

In summary then, use Part 1 (or check out the Key Points on pages 12–13) to remind yourself of the general process and approach.

Refer to Part 2 for ways to collect information, Part 3 on how to analyse information and Part 4 to find a solution.

Part 5 will provide ideas on how to improve your chances of success.

PART 1

# What is Problem Solving?

The simple answer to this question may seem to be something along the lines of 'deciding what to do in a difficult situation'.

This implies that when faced with a problem we think about it for a few minutes, weigh up a few facts and then make a decision. This is indeed what people do, thousands of times every day, with varying degrees of success. Most of the problems we have to solve are relatively simple and unimportant.

- This payment is overdue – should I write to or phone the debtor?
- It is foggy – should I drive or take the train?
- The fax machine needs replacing – should we rent or buy?

Normally we make our decisions about such problems in very little time and often with no conscious analysis of the facts. We may at the same time feel that we have carried out some hard-headed calculations, particularly where money is involved, but it is often the case that the 'analysis' was overridden and influenced by intuitive or emotional factors.

Replacing the fax machine provides a case in point. We might take the trouble to find out the tax implications of rental or purchase and work out cost comparisons if the machine lasts two, three, four years or whatever. We might take into account the differences in maintenance costs and we might also explore the various leasing alternatives available to us.

The likelihood is that we will do none of these things however, but will make a quick decision based on:

- the fact that we are very busy;
- our unchallenged policy of purchasing and not renting; or
- our reluctance to fork out a lump sum.

Alternatively, our problem may be one we have solved before, perhaps on many occasions. If our plastics injection moulding machine is not turning out products of adequate quality we may, with little conscious thought, adjust the temperature or pressure to achieve the desired result. This, perhaps, we have done many times before.

The speed with which we can make such decisions can give the impression that problem solving is an event, when it is in fact a process.

The recognition and disciplined application of the process are vital when faced with a really significant problem. The damage which might arise from taking the wrong decision could be fatal to the business in extreme cases or at least make the problem worse in others.

This process, which will be outlined in this chapter and covered in detail later, is an essential requirement when faced with problems such as:

- abandoning rather than modifying a long-established 'bread and butter' product which is showing signs of losing its competitiveness;
- making some skilled people redundant when a recession begins to bite – and knowing that there will be a shortage of skilled staff when the recession is over;
- deciding whether to close down a factory needing a substantial injection of capital investment to keep a good product price-competitive;
- finding that a major customer who owes a substantial sum for goods already supplied is showing signs of going bust.

Making a decision in such cases involves significant risk to any business and anything less than a disciplined and systematic approach is certainly irresponsible and could result in disaster.

The problem-solving process involves the following four stages.

## Stage 1 Identifying and defining the problem

Problems can easily be confused with symptoms. The classic case is that of the manager who cannot achieve his objectives because of 'shortage of staff'. The knee-jerk reaction to many business difficulties is to put it down to a shortage of staff. The symptoms often point this way and can include:

- backlogs of work;
- persistent overtime working;
- delays in meeting customers' needs;
- staff stress and low morale;

- poor quality work;
- failure to meet output targets.

Given such difficulties a manager may well insist that his problem is that he does not have enough people, but in fact the poor performance could be the result of:

- a badly designed computer system;
- lack of a monitoring system;
- inadequate communications (e.g. staff do not know what is expected of them);
- poor work planning;
- an out-of-date organisation structure;
- incompetent supervisors;

or any number of other underlying causes. If this is the case the addition of more people (at some cost) may only marginally improve matters – or may not improve them at all, while the real and unidentified problem will remain undetected and unchanged.

Sometimes the real problem can be rapidly identified as a result of some brief examination of the available facts, often including asking employees what, in their opinion, is the cause of the trouble. Or sometimes the problem can be uncovered by asking the questions, 'What are we trying to do?' and 'What should we be trying to do?' It is not unknown for a situation to be an apparent problem when in fact the objective itself is wrong or has been overtaken by events.

In many such cases the 'problem' can, with some thought, be turned into an opportunity.

Such a situation was well illustrated by a company where the head of a division unexpectedly resigned. There was much wailing and gnashing of teeth as the company worked on the apparent problem of finding a replacement. There was no one in the company with sufficient know-how and experience, and much time (and cash) was spent searching the job market. Having failed to find a suitable replacement someone asked, 'Do we *have* to find a replacement?' This question, which at first seemed rather silly, gave rise to more thought. The outcome was a decision to disband the whole division and allocate its work to other parts of the company. This should have been done long before, but had not been done simply because no one had thought to challenge the status quo. This illustrates another feature of the business of identifying the problem. Is it a problem just because we are used to a given situation and/or are we in the *habit* of doing things in a particular way?

The specific objectives of management must be clearly established or re-established if there is to be any consistent success in problem solving. For example, will management prefer to maintain leadership of its market even if this means reducing prices and profits? Would it be better to sacrifice short-term profit for long-term gain? The objective (possibly continued market domination) must be clear if the right alternative choice of action is to be agreed. A decision to maintain prices and profits might endanger the objective of maintaining market leadership in the long term.

## Stage 2 Collecting information

The more information which is available to decision makers the easier it will be to reach a decision – and one which most effectively solves the problem.

If you are aware of the costs of alternative lines of action, the number of customers using certain types of machines, the effect of a change in interest rates or anything else relevant to the problem then finding the solution is easier. This may sound obvious but too many important business decisions are taken without adequate fact finding. There are many reasons for this which all managers will have experienced at some time, e.g.:

- there is not enough time to obtain the information before action must be taken;
- the information is difficult or impossible to obtain;
- the information available is of doubtful accuracy (perhaps it is out of date).

In such cases an intuitive, gut-feel response is the likely result and this may indeed be the best approach. How to make the best use of limited or imperfect information, combined with experience and intuition, is described in Part 4.

However, every effort should be made to collect as much information as possible. It may completely change the situation and cause the problem to 'go away' of its own volition.

> There were severe delays for a business, when setting up a subsidiary company in Sweden, in drafting sales contracts in Swedish. The lawyers were taking their time and the deadline for starting business was rapidly approaching. The wording of the contract was urgently needed by the printers and pressure was being put on the lawyers to speed things up. It was then discovered that the English language version, already available and in use elsewhere, was acceptable to Swedish customers and actually preferred by many of them!
>
> The problem vanished overnight.
>
> Assumptions in business are often convenient and frequently dangerous. The assumption that a Swedish language contract was essential could have delayed the start of business.

The convenience of an assumption is gained from the fact that if we can convince ourselves that it is valid then we avoid the necessity to check it out. This is very tempting when we are under pressure. Furthermore, assumptions passed from one person to another tend to be translated into 'facts'.

Assumptions can come in all shapes and sizes and may include the following examples:

> 'The customer will never agree to that idea.'
> 'The costs will be too high.'
> 'We will not be able to get the staff in over the weekend.'

and, of course,

> 'Our Swedish customers will insist on a Swedish language contract.'

Assumptions tend to influence our behaviour and, in negotiations, can cause us to take a less bullish approach. In turn, this can cause us to accept a less favourable outcome. Assumptions can lead us to taking no action or the wrong action when, for the sake of a little fact finding, the whole situation could have been turned to our advantage.

Sometimes, as was illustrated in the Swedish example, the information collected will immediately point to the solution to the problem. However, in many cases things are not so easy. Major strategic decisions may require the analysis of masses of data, sometimes of varying quality. In such cases a third problem-solving stage is required.

## Stage 3 Analysing the information

Proper analysis requires the use of the right technique, i.e. one which is relevant and statistically or otherwise valid.

Ideally the simplest possible technique(s) should be used and every effort made to avoid being bogged down in yards of computer printout and complex formulae. There are times, however, when a technique such as mathematical modelling will be needed and every manager worthy of the name should have a working knowledge of such methods. Fortunately the availability of modern computer software often removes the need for the manager to be an expert in the esoterics.

Some of the more down-to-earth techniques are described in Part 2. These have been chosen to be of practical use to the manager who does not have statisticians or other experts at hand to help him to make the choice between alternative courses of action. This is likely to apply to the majority of managers.

It is important to recognise that the information you collect may not be wholly reliable. Even if it is the subsequent analysis will inevitably result in conclusions which will be used to decide *future* action. The appropriateness of this action will rely on the accuracy of forecasts of what will happen. Forecasts are by definition uncertain and should not be regarded as prophecies.

This is not, however, an argument for doing nothing on the grounds that we cannot, with certainty, foretell the future. In fact, this uncertainty is the very reason why every scrap of information should be taken into account so that the manager has more to go on than a guess. Failure to attempt a forecast based on what is known means that the manager will be at the mercy of whatever comes along, and will be unprepared and only able to react on a day-to-day basis. In other words he or she will be controlled by events rather than the reverse.

## Stage 4 Preparing a plan of action

The result of the analysis stage should be a decision on which a plan of action can be constructed to resolve the problem.

Depending on the nature of the problem the plan could be simple or complex, short term or long term. In every case your plan should have the following characteristics. It should be:

- wholly relevant to the problem and not adulterated by add-ons to achieve other purposes;
- based on a timetable of action by specified individuals;
- capable of revision if and when results of the action taken indicate that a change is necessary;
- compatible with company or departmental objectives;
- thoroughly communicated to all concerned.

If the plan does not have these characteristics it is likely that things will go wrong – or, and it happens – action which should be taken will not be taken.

## Key points

1. Problem solving is a process rather than an event.
2. Effective problem solving demands the implementation of a process which is comprised of four stages:

   - identifying and defining the problem;
   - collecting information relating to the problem;
   - analysing the information and reaching a decision;
   - implementing the action required.

3. Even the smallest problem requires each of the four steps to be taken, although in minor cases this is likely to be done almost unconsciously.

4. Symptoms of the problem must not be confused with the problem itself. Nor must assumptions be made about the cause of the problem or its solution.

5. Sometimes identifying and defining the problem can cause it to 'go away', for example when, after some consideration, the objective to be achieved is changed.

6. Collecting the information can also result in the problem 'going away' or an opportunity can be revealed causing the company to change direction which leaves the problem behind.

7. Even the most careful examination of the problem, collection of data and analysis may come to nothing if implementation of a plan is neglected. A plan which meets a number of criteria is essential – however simple that plan may be.

## PART 2

# Ways to Collect the Information You Need

The method you choose for getting at the facts which lie behind your problem will depend on the type of problem you are facing. Some of the techniques described below have wide application and can be used in a variety of circumstances. Others are appropriate for more specific situations. To provide a general guide, suggestions are made, for each of the techniques described, of the type of problem to which the techniques might be applied.

It may not always be possible to obtain all the information ideally required and some of the information collected may be out of date or otherwise less than perfect. This should not discourage you from going ahead. Partial information is better than none at all and provided that a measure of common sense is applied when analysing the information (i.e. making some allowances for likely error), progress can still be made.

A common mistake is to spend time and money in an attempt to achieve a level of accuracy which is unnecessary and sometimes illusory, for example, a business decision which depends on knowing the price of something is not likely to be different if the amount is £1000, £990, £1010 or £995.60. It is often the order of magnitude which matters and the answer that something will cost approximately £1000 will result in the same decision as if the answer had been £995.60. Care should also be taken to avoid the trap of taking a number of estimated values, perhaps combining them with more certain information, and then doing a calculation to a number of decimal places. This results in an illusory impression of total reliability and has been the cause of many disappointments. This mistake has even been made by certain insurance underwriters – who should know better.

Armed with these caveats we will now take a look at some of the information-gathering techniques you should consider.

# 1. SYSTEMS STUDY

Not to be confused with computer systems analysis, systems study has wide application. Symptoms which suggest that you should use it include:

- paperwork delays and bureaucratic errors;
- delays in production and distribution;
- high labour costs in administration functions;
- slow billing and collection of debts;
- slow and/or expensive estimating and preparation of quotations.

The essence of the technique is finding out what goes on, and is based on asking four simple questions.

'What is being done – and why?'
'Who is doing it – and why?'
'When is it done – and why?'
'Where is it done – and why?'

Persistent probing using these questions can result in some well-worn answers and also some surprises. Common answers include:

'We have always done it this way.'
'Mr Tompkins (who died 18 years ago) said we should do it.'
'I don't know why.'

All these answers suggest that improvements can be made. Surprise answers you may get are illustrated by the following real-life cases.

- Time and money spent in preparing a routine report for a director who did not want it – but had never said so.
- A card index record of stock levels which was kept long after a computer system had been installed. No one had ever told the storekeeper to drop the record.
- Product packing carried out in a building some distance from the production line (because it was always done that way), when it could and should have been done at the end of the

production line. No one had ever challenged the arrangement which caused delays, muddle and sometimes damage.

Having asked the questions – and cross-checked the answers – some form of 'display' is needed so that the wood can be seen from the trees.

Two simple approaches work well in most cases to illustrate what is going on and to provide a guide to useful change.

## The work examination chart

The chart shown in Figure 2.1 is based on the four questions set out earlier.

Having examined what goes on, and where, when and how things are done, the work examination chart can be filled in. The two left-hand columns are used to record the results of the investigation. It may, at first sight, appear pedantic to fill in these columns but doing so has two clear advantages.

- The form summarises and makes clearer what could be quite a lot of information recorded in note form during the investigation.
- Completion of the boxes ensures that the investigation has been fully carried out and that all the subjects have been addressed.

The third column, recording the alternatives to what happens now, requires some thinking and imagination to complete. You should keep this third column in mind during the investigation stage as alternatives can often be suggested by the people doing the work – especially if prompted to do so.

In the fourth column the decision as to what changes to make to resolve the problem are recorded.

So, the work examination chart thus covers all the first three stages of problem solving. You may even find that the result of systems study extends beyond fact finding to obtaining the answer to the problem – if the action required is fairly obvious.

| | What is achieved? | Why is it done? | Is there an alternative? | What changes should be made? |
|---|---|---|---|---|
| PURPOSE OF THE WORK | | | | |
| | Where? | Why there? | Is there an alternative? | Is there a better place? |
| THE PLACE | | | | |
| | When? | Why then? | Can it be done at another time? | When should it be done? |
| THE WORK SEQUENCE | | | | |
| | Who does it? | Why these people? | Can anyone else do it? | Who should do it? |
| THE PEOPLE INVOLVED | | | | |
| | How is it done? | Why that way? | How otherwise could it be done? | How should it be done? |
| THE MEANS | | | | |

*Figure 2.1* Work examination chart

A completed form may look something like the example shown in figure 2.2.

In the hypothetical case shown in Figure 2.2 there might have been a problem of delays in producing the policy documents that clients were waiting for. The investigation showed that the delays were caused by:

- waiting until the debit note was completed;
- using typewriters (when word processors were available).

Although hypothetical, this example is based on a real-life case where delays were caused by the sequence of the work. Job A was not done until Job B was completed. This was an unnecessary constraint going back into the mists of time when perhaps there was a good reason for the sequence being used. Circumstances change, but the system will often remain the same. Systems study and the work examination chart will often reveal faults like this.

## Using a flow chart

A flow chart is the second way to illustrate what is going on and as often as not it is worth preparing one in addition to a work examination chart.

In particular, a flow chart will show the sequence of events allowing the investigators to ask questions like this.

- 'Why does a copy of the invoice go to the planning office?'
- 'Everything has to be checked and approved by the deputy accountant. Why?'
- 'Why are faulty widgets stored off-site?'
- 'What is the purpose of the second quality check if goods have passed the first one?'

There are a variety of types and styles of flow chart, but they are all based on the same principles, which are:

- to indicate action and where it takes place;
- to indicate delays and non-action;
- to reveal movements of work and/or goods.

| | **What is achieved?** | **Why is it done?** | **Is there an alternative?** | **What changes should be made?** |
|---|---|---|---|---|
| **PURPOSE OF THE WORK** | *Preparation of insurance policy clauses* | *To complete the policy* | *No* | *None* |
| | **Where?** | **Why there?** | **Is there an alternative?** | **Is there a better place?** |
| **THE PLACE** | *Brokers' office* | *Nearest to broker responsible* | *Anywhere in the building* | *Secretaries' office* |
| | **When?** | **Why then?** | **Can it be done at another time?** | **When should it be done?** |
| **THE WORK SEQUENCE** | *After debit note completed* | *Always done it after debit note* | *Yes, before debit note would save time* | *Before debit note* |
| | **Who does it?** | **Why these people?** | **Can anyone else do it?** | **Who should do it?** |
| **THE PEOPLE INVOLVED** | *Assistant brokers* | *No clear reason* | *Anyone who can type* | *Secretaries* |
| | **How is it done?** | **Why that way?** | **How otherwise could it be done?** | **How should it be done?** |
| **THE MEANS** | *Typewriter* | *Must have typed documents* | *Word processor* | *Using existing word processor* |

*Figure 2.2* Completed work examination chart

One of the best types of flow chart uses columns to represent the activity (or lack of it) in different departments. A simple example is shown in figure 2.3.

Figure 2.3 shows the familiar situation where, on completion of a batch of product, both the test department and production planning are informed by means of a copy of a batch note.

The problems which need to be solved could be that:

**a.** testing does not take place soon enough and despatch is held up; or

**b.** production planning are advised that the batch has been completed but cannot use it as they have no test results – until later. They are therefore not able to promptly re-schedule production if a batch is faulty.

The flow chart reveals the causes of the delay, i.e.:

- a sample is not taken until *after* the batch reaches the warehouse;
- further time is lost in the test department in marrying the right batch note with the sample before testing can begin.

It is likely that in real life from time to time a batch note will be 'lost', a sample overlooked, or production planning will take a chance and assume (hopefully) that the batch is a good one and plan accordingly.

The solution could be to take a sample before the batch goes to the warehouse and to send the sample *with* the batch note to the test department. In addition, production planning should be advised by the test department of completion of the batch.

## *Treating the symptoms*

In a similar real-life case arrangements were made for production planning to be advised of completion of product *prior to test* because of delays. The *cause* of the delay was not investigated and corrected at the time, so the information sent to production planning was potentially misleading.

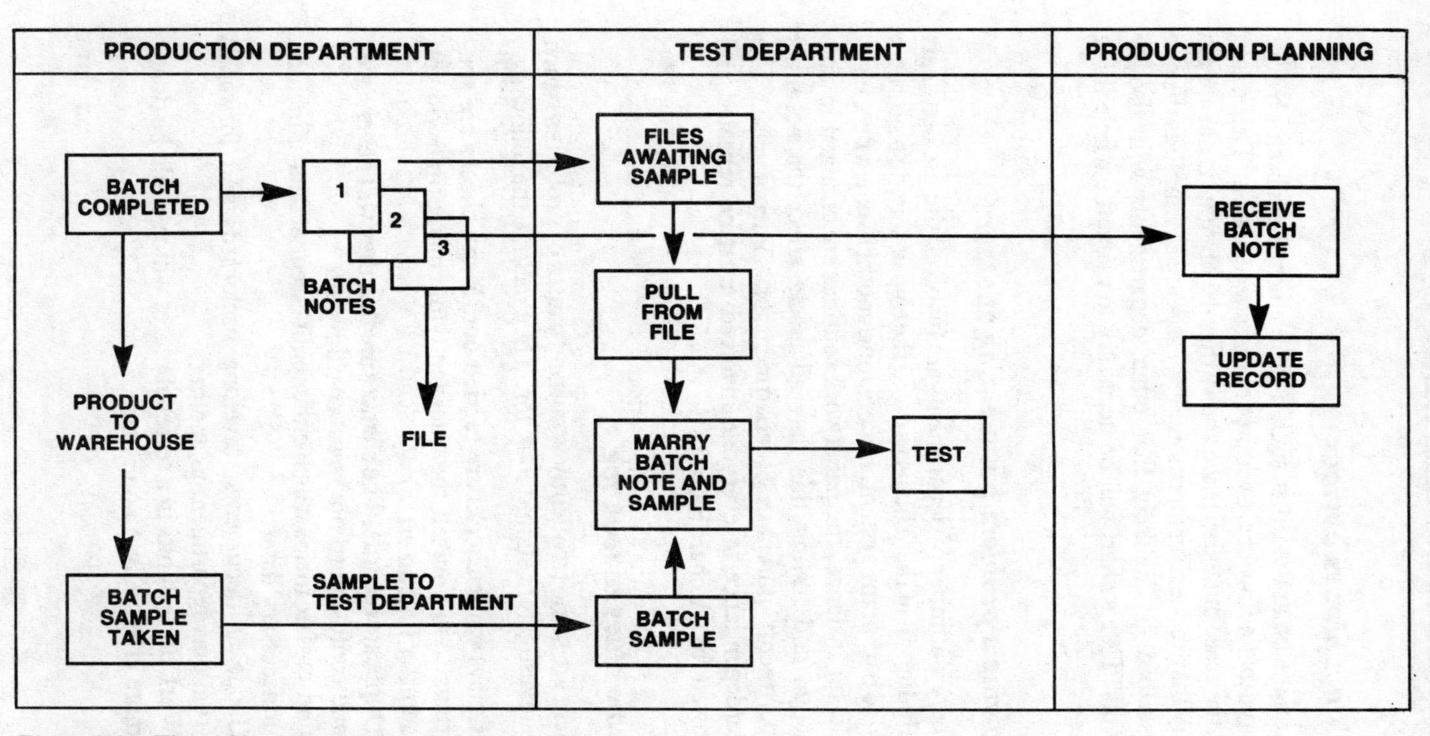


*Figure 2.3* Flow chart: production and testing

## *It's not always obvious*

It might be argued that such a problem had such an obvious cause that a flow chart was not necessary to spot it. This might be the case, but experience shows that the obvious is not always very easy to see. Furthermore, few cases are as simple as the one described. It is likely that other departments will also be involved, so a chart will be necessary to make the whole thing clear.

## *Solving a problem but creating another*

Where a number of departments are involved the use of a chart including all of them helps to avoid the trap of solving a problem in one part of the system, but creating another somewhere else.

If, for instance, the paperwork routines are changed in production and testing this may adversely affect the accounts department, purchasing department or someone else. The interdependence of everyone involved must be revealed and allowed for. A chart helps to do this.

## *Some clues to look for*

There are some frequently occurring causes of problems which the investigators should look for. They include the following.

- Delays while checks are carried out. Many checks are spurious. Ask yourself the question 'How many times do you actually find an error?'
- Duplicate records. The chances are that they will never agree and confusion (if not rows) could result.
- Out-of-date forms which either omit essential data or include unnecessary data.
- Goods or documents travelling backwards and forwards from one department to another.
- Work done in bits in a series of places which could be done, more effectively, in one place.

# 2. VALUE ANALYSIS

Value analysis is an old technique which was undoubtedly practised long before it was given a name. It became prominent in the engineering world in the 1950s and 1960s, but was also found to have applications in marketing and other non-engineering activities.

Essentially, the purpose of value analysis is to identify and eliminate all the unnecessary costs associated with a business activity. This can include:

- the design of a product;
- specifications for goods or services being purchased;
- marketing activities, e.g. a stand at a trade exhibition;
- the design and equipping of a prestige office building.

In short, the technique can be employed wherever cost is a problem – particularly in developing a new product which must compete in a tough market.

It is applicable to both minor and simple problems, such as where the cost of producing a sales brochure is greater than the budget allows, or to major problems such as where an important product is costing more to manufacture than was allowed for when setting the price.

## How does value analysis work?

This technique is based on a series of questions, some of which will be about the nature of the problem and some about the features of the product or activity under examination.

The purpose of asking these questions is to:

- draw attention to cost-saving possibilities; and
- identify the cost-saving possibilities with a practical application.

A 'standard' set of questions is listed below, which you may wish to modify to suit your circumstances.

## The questions to ask

1. What is it that we are trying to do (or produce)?
2. What are the absolute essential minimum requirements?
3. What is the customer looking for?
4. Are there any aspects of our scheme which, if changed, will be entirely acceptable to customers?
5. Is there anything in our design or intentions which is contrary to or exceeds the answers to Questions 1 to 4?
6. What (such as processes or features) can we remove from our plan or specification which will reduce cost, but not reduce the utilitarian value of the plan or specification?
7. Are there any alternatives to the proposed features of our scheme which would be cheaper but equally effective?
8. Can any standards be reduced without damaging effectiveness?
9. Can the product or idea actually be improved by removing or reducing the cost of some feature of it?

It will be seen that asking these questions is a way of challenging what has so far been accepted as necessary or desirable.

## A classic case

An American company had supplied a product to a major customer for many years. The product had been designed to provide a high level of resistance to wear and this feature was costly to provide. When, resulting from problems of holding prices down, the customer was questioned, it was revealed that the level of wear resistance was actually unnecessarily high. Using value analysis the question 'Can wear resistance be reduced?' was asked.

## Victorian folly?

An example of a failure to carry out value analysis can be seen in many Victorian office buildings. These are often constructed with decorative embellishments – even including scrollwork and the like which are invisible to a person standing in the street, and imposing but unnecessarily large entrance lobbies and the like. While there was no doubt an element of image creation associated with these buildings, it was likely that vast sums were expended unnecessarily and not always artistically. In more cost-conscious times value analysis might well have resulted in some design changes.

## Some examples of value analysis at work

The following real-life examples illustrate the kind of results that can be achieved using value analysis.

- Packing a product in a 3-ply paper sack rather than the 4-ply sack used before. The reduced protection was more than adequate – and cheaper.
- Abandoning the idea of a very upmarket and expensive reception area. It was agreed that no business would be lost by using a more utilitarian design. It was also argued that some customers would be discouraged by a display of opulence which might suggest unnecessarily high prices.
- Replacing an expensively printed invoice (on high-quality paper) with something more ordinary. Fancy invoices, it was agreed, did not encourage more orders or earlier payment.
- Abandoning the drilling of holes in a metal casting. The holes were intended to reduce the weight of the casting, but when challenged it was agreed that this was not, in fact, necessary.

In all these cases problems of cost were solved by asking the right questions and acquiring information in one way or another.

# 3. REGRESSION ANALYSIS

If we knew what was going to happen in the future, many of our problems would immediately be over. For this reason statisticians and others have expended much time and energy on devising forecasting techniques. Some of the forecasting methods developed are fairly complex and involve the kind of mathematics with which only a minority of business people are familiar.

Regression analysis, which can be used in certain cases to provide us with a forecast, does not necessarily require a mathematical approach. There is one of course and if you are interested you should look up the 'linear regression coefficient' in a statistics textbook. That is if the very name does not make you shudder!

Fortunately, busy managers can opt for the easier way.

## When should regression analysis be used?

There are times when the ways in which, say, sales are developing or machine breakdown occurrences arise are unclear. If you look at the figures involved, there appears to be no obvious trend. This can have a bearing on problems such as whether:

- to invest or not to invest;
- to carry out more or less preventive maintenance;
- to employ more staff or not.

Regression analysis provides a way to spot any concealed trend and the technique can be used in a very quick and easy way.

## Are sales up, down or steady?

Imagine a situation where sales over a twelve-month period have been as follows:

| | | | |
|---|---|---|---|
| JAN. | 650 | | |
| FEB. | 750 | | |
| MAR. | 600 | | |
| APR. | 500 | | |
| MAY | 550 | | |
| JUNE | 850 | Average sales | 571 |
| JULY | 350 | | |
| AUG. | 550 | | |
| SEPT. | 500 | | |
| OCT. | 500 | | |
| NOV | 600 | | |
| DEC. | 450 | | |

Assuming that there are no seasonal factors to take into account it is not easy to see whether there is a trend up, down or none at all.

The good result in June was followed by a very poor result in July and although the November figure was above average, December sales were down again. Although January and Febrary sales were quite good, March sales were no better than November's result. So, what is happening?

A clearer picture might emerge if the figures were to be plotted on to a graph as is shown in figure 2.4.

In fact the graph alone does not help very much. The scatter of plots is fairly wide, especially the June and July months which 'contradict' each other. What is now needed is the so-called regression line.

## *Using a regression line*

First, work out the average of all the values – in this case 571. Mark the average on the graph at the mid-way point on the time scale, i.e. between June and July.

This can be seen as a cross on the graph in figure 2.5.

Next take a transparent ruler or a length of thread and place it on the graph so that it (a) passes through the cross marking the central point and (b) best fits the plots with about equal numbers of points above and below – making allowances for any

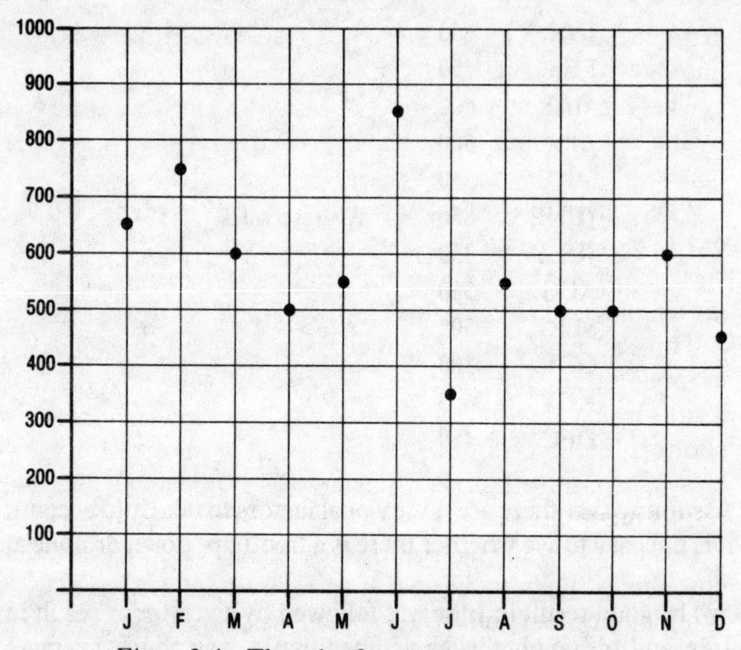


*Figure 2.4* The sales figures plotted on a graph

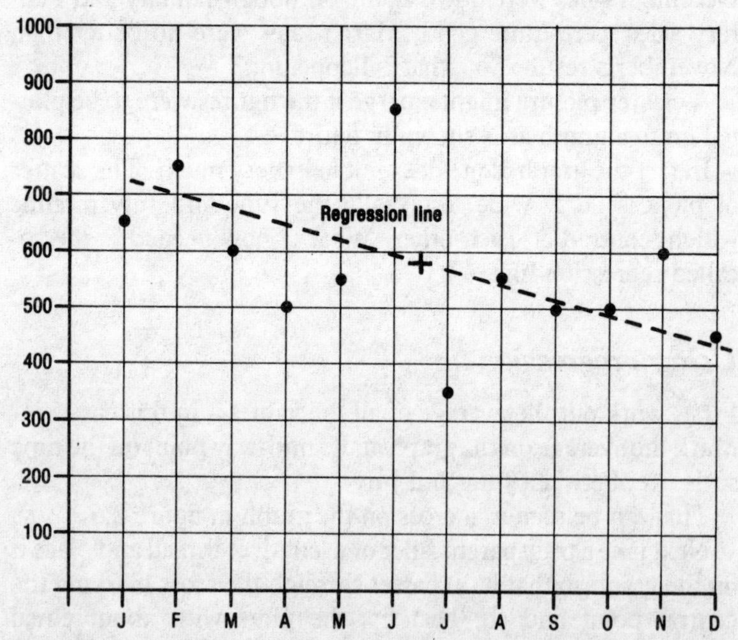


*Figure 2.5* The central point and regression line marked on the graph

extreme figures. The result should be something like the dotted line shown in Figure 2.5.

The line indicates a distinct trend downwards, emphasised by the fact that four of the last five points are very close to the regression line.

This does not necessarily mean that the results of the next two or three months will be close to an extension of the line. The variations from month to month are likely to continue, but *on the information available* there is an overall downward trend.

This somewhat crude method must be used sensibly. For example, allowance may have to be made for any month's results which are a long way out of line, but for which there is a clear explanation. If the cause is a one-off (a rail strike, a warehouse fire or something similar), then the average of all the other results might be used, instead of the odd-ball figure.

If you find a trend in your figures you may well want to know how this is likely to affect you in future and to what extent. Working out the 'standard deviation' can help you to discover this.

# 4. THE STANDARD DEVIATION

If you have some past figures to go on, the standard deviation (don't be put off by this statisticians' label) can give you some idea of what is likely to be the future situation. But, remember, this can only be a forecast and not the result of using an infallible crystal ball.

## What is standard deviation?

The mathematicians' definition is 'A measure of the scatter of a series of numbers about their mean value. It is the square root of the average value of the squares of the deviations from their mean value.'

The best way to translate this into layman's terms is to work through an example. We will take the last six months' figures from our regression line example.

| | | |
|---|---|---|
| JULY | 350 | |
| AUG. | 550 | |
| SEPT. | 500 | |
| OCT. | 500 | |
| NOV. | 600 | |
| DEC. | 450 | |
| **TOTAL** | 2950 | **Average** 492 (to nearest whole number) |

Having worked out the average we can now, by subtraction, calculate the *variance* from the average in each case, thus resulting in a second column. We can also square each of the variances giving us a third column.

| | | Variance | Variances squared |
|---|---|---|---|
| JULY | 350 | –142 | 20 164 |
| AUG. | 550 | 58 | 3364 |
| SEPT. | 500 | 8 | 64 |
| OCT. | 500 | 8 | 64 |
| NOV. | 600 | 108 | 11 664 |
| DEC. | 450 | – 42 | 1764 |
| **TOTAL** | 2950 | | **TOTAL** 37 084 |
| **AVERAGE** | 492 | | |

The next step is to calculate the average of the total from the third column – but an average with a small difference. This is that the total of the squared variances is divided not by the number of values in the series (6), but by one less (5).

This gives a figure of 37084 ÷ 5 = 7417. The square root of 7417 is **86**. So, this is the standard deviation.

## What does the standard deviation mean?

There can be no guarantee that the variables in a series of past figures will be exactly the same in a future series. However, business results do not often change suddenly and dramatically, and the standard deviation enables us to forecast the range in which future figures will lie.

The 'rule' is that about 70 per cent of future values will fall within one standard deviation of the average. In other words, about 70 per cent will be in the range 492 plus or minus 86. About 95 per cent of future results will be in the range 492 plus or minus 2 standard deviation.

This can give some very helpful guidance. Suppose, for example, that you suspect a downward trend in your sales. This, if it continues, could have serious implications for cash-flow, stock levels, purchasing, advertising and so on. You will have the problem of making adjustments or taking 'emergency' action – but to what extent? It is easy either to overreact or the reverse in such situations.

Having some idea of what the *range* of future results is likely to be can guide you to the right degree of reaction.

# 5. THE BREAK-EVEN POINT

A simple concept and often not all that difficult to work out, the break-even point is one of the most useful items of information a business can have.

The break-even point is that point, e.g. level of sales, at which the revenue earned exactly matches the fixed and variable costs incurred. Any level of business below the break-even point will be loss-making, but any level above it will result in a profit. Clearly, knowing what has to be done to make a profit is vital. However, the use of the break-even point does not end there. It can be used as a guide when considering the expansion (or contraction) of the business, investing in more machinery, vehicles or equipment and any other action which will result in a significant change of costs.

## Working it out – an example

Suppose you are a solicitor running a successful practice in a country town. You rent a modest office, employ a secretary and pay for a fax machine, photocopier and office supplies.

Your income and expenses work out as follows:

| **Expenditure** | **£** |
|---|---|
| Office rent | 6000 p.a. |
| Secretary | 12 000 p.a. |
| **Total fixed costs** | 18 000 p.a. |

You also incur variable costs such as office supplies, telephone, etc., which depend on how much work you do. The amount works out at £5 per fee-earning hour.

Your variable costs, based on 880 fee-earning hours per year work out at £4400.

Your total expenditure is £18 000 + £4400 = £22 400.

| **Income** | **£** |
|---|---|
| Fees earned | 44 400 |

The income is based on working the 880 fee earning-hours @ £50 per hour.

You now have reason to believe that you can expand your business, but in order to take on more work you must (a) move into larger, more expensive premises and (b) employ a legal clerk.

Your expenditure, if you do this, will be:

| | **£** |
|---|---|
| Office rent | 12 000 p.a. |
| Clerk | 15 000 p.a. |
| Secretary | 12 000 p.a. |
| **Total fixed costs** | 39 000 p.a. |

Clearly, unless your income rises, you will make a loss at the present levels of work. The problem is to decide whether or not to go ahead. Assuming that the level of fee charged cannot be increased, how many fee-earning hours must be worked to break even and make various levels of profit?

The fixed and variable cost can now be put into a table (2.1) against varying levels of fee earning.

Examination of the table shows that under the new arrangements a loss would be made at a level of 800 fee-earning hours and a small profit made at 900 hours. The break-even point lies in between. If, in fact, the same 880 hours were worked the result would be £44 400–£43 400 = £600 profit.

In order to earn the same profit as before (£21 600) it will be necessary to increase fee earning hours to an amount exceeding 1300 hours.

You now know where you stand and must decide the following.

- Is it likely that you can expand your business sufficiently to achieve, say, 1300 fee-earning hours?

| Fee-earning hours | Fixed costs £ | Variable costs £ | Total costs £ | Income costs £ | Profit (loss) £ |
|---|---|---|---|---|---|
| 500 | 39 000 | 2500 | 41 500 | 25 000 | (16 500) |
| 600 | 39 000 | 3000 | 42 000 | 30 000 | (12 000) |
| 700 | 39 000 | 3500 | 42 500 | 35 000 | ( 7500) |
| 800 | 39 000 | 4000 | 43 000 | 40 000 | ( 3000) |
| 900 | 39 000 | 4500 | 43 500 | 45 000 | 1500 |
| 1000 | 39 000 | 5000 | 44 000 | 50 000 | 6000 |
| 1100 | 39 000 | 5500 | 44 500 | 55 000 | 10 500 |
| 1200 | 39 000 | 6000 | 45 000 | 60 000 | 15 000 |
| 1300 | 39 000 | 6500 | 45 500 | 65 000 | 19 500 |
| 1400 | 39 000 | 7000 | 46 000 | 70 000 | 24 000 |
| 1500 | 39 000 | 7500 | 46 500 | 75 000 | 28 500 |
| 1600 | 39 000 | 8000 | 47 000 | 80 000 | 33 000 |

*Table 2.1* Fixed and variable costs

- To what extent will the presence of the clerk increase your capacity?

Knowing what must be achieved still leaves such questions unanswered, but at least the facts can be set against a view as to what is feasible.

One company, reacting to increasing business, took on more staff and a new, larger office. They did not work out the effect on their fixed costs and later found to their cost that increases in revenue did not cover them. The break-even point had been raised to a point where a loss was inevitable in the short to medium term.

## Using a graph

Your figures showing costs and revenue at varying levels of activity can be usefully displayed in graph form. This will give you an easy to assimilate picture of what will be the result of alternative courses of action.

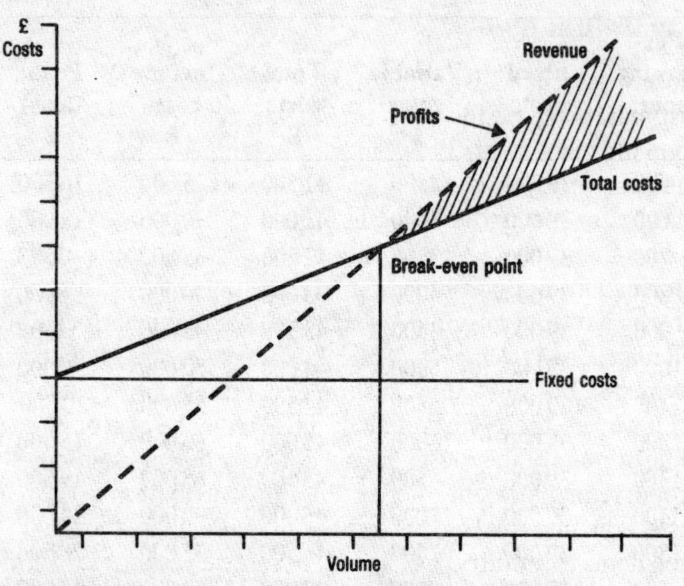


*Figure 2.6* A break-even point graph

The break-even point occurs where revenue equals the sum of the fixed costs and the variable costs.

The fixed costs in Figure 2.6 remain the same throughout. With an expansion of activity the fixed costs often, at some point, will increase and this will have the effect of moving the break-even point to the right on the graph – which will now show what new volume must be achieved.

> *NOTE:* In real life fixed costs frequently go up in steps and not, as the graph implies, gradually. The change from profit to loss can be instant!

Preparing a series of graphs to illustrate a variety of possible scenarios can put the problem into perspective and provide some numbers to work with.

In addition to providing information on what will happen if expansion takes place a break-even calculation can be used to:

- show what will happen if prices are increased (assuming volumes do not suffer); and
- show the effects of cutting costs.

## A marginal point

Closely associated with the break-even point is the marginal cost/marginal revenue concept. The break-even point depends upon the relationship between costs and revenue, as volumes of business go up or down. Each movement subtracts or adds a 'margin' of cost and a 'margin' of revenue.

The marginal cost or revenue can be a valuable piece of information. Suppose, for example, an hotel has a vacant room for which it would normally charge £50 per night. This charge is calculated to cover a range of fixed costs such as mortgage payments, business rates, insurances and telephone rentals.

However, these costs will be incurred whether or not all, some or none of the rooms are occupied by paying customers. If a room remains vacant, there will be no contribution to the fixed costs. The marginal cost of letting the room will be made up of such items as laundry, a bar of soap, some electricity consumption and other small costs. If these costs add up to, say, £5 then it would pay the hotel owner to let the room at any price exceeding £5. The difference will be a *contribution* to fixed costs but this, of course, will not amount to a profit.

Understanding the marginal cost of any service or product can be valuable in enabling otherwise wasted assets to be used at least as a means to reduce losses. There will naturally be other factors to take into account – for example, not upsetting the market by offering such reduced prices as could set a dangerous precedent.

However, there are situations where it can pay off, as in the case of a small manufacturing company. Business was patchy and the owners found that they had periods of time when resources were not fully utilised – but fixed costs were unchanged. They found that they could produce and sell goods which did not compete with their normal line. These goods could not be sold at prices which covered all the variable plus fixed costs. The marginal cost was calculated and found to be less than the price which could be obtained, and so contributed to paying for the fixed costs essential to the mainstream business. By using the slack time to produce these alternative products, cash was earned to help pay for the fixed costs.

# 6. ACTIVITY SAMPLING

In the bad old days businesses used to employ so-called efficiency experts. These experts would stand around with clipboards and stop-watches noting what people did and timing them.

Fortunately, there is a better way to find out what goes on – which avoids all the adverse effects of having 'company spies' lurking in dark corners. This technique is activity sampling, which involves the employees and puts them in the driving seat. This encourages co-operation, accuracy of the data gathered and commitment to any resulting decisions.

## What can activity sampling be used for?

It is frequently the case that solving a problem depends on knowing the answer to questions such as the following.

- How many people are needed to do a certain job?
- How many times does something happen – in a day, a week or whatever?
- The labour cost of work which is mixed with other work done by the same people.
- The reason why there are hold-ups and delays in getting something done.
- The amount of someone's time taken up by certain activities.

Sometimes there are records which will tell you the answer, but often there are not – or the records, which were not designed for the purpose, may be misleading.

You could ask the employees directly, but this can result in the wrong answer. This is not necessarily because all employees are untruthful. Wrong answers tend to come from employees because their memories fail them and they, quite naturally, are often subjective.

If you ask a clerk what takes up most of his time he or she is likely to name the work which is more aggravating or which he or she most dislikes. Actual measurement often shows that such work, although prominent in the mind of the employee, takes much less time than he or she thought. Activity sampling eliminates this distortion.

## How does activity sampling work?

The best way to answer this question is to work through the process which starts, continues and ends with the close involvement of the employees concerned.

### *Step 1*

The problem to be solved is carefully defined and explained, in full, to the employees. Everyone should know why a fact-finding study is being carried out and reassured that it is not a fault-finding expedition or some form of witch-hunt. What is to happen and why must be fully communicated.

### *Step 2*

Discuss with each person involved in the work being studied the nature of what they do. The purpose of this stage is to identify their main tasks. A production planner for example, is likely to list the following activities:

- examining sales forecasts;
- calculating raw material requirements;
- preparing machine schedules;
- liaising with purchasing department;
- preparing production reports, and so on.

### *Step 3*

Having identified the main activities, a form is completed for each employee, listing their activities and also including provision for associated, but not necessarily stated, activities. The form will also be completed with a series of *random* times of the day. It will look something like the form in Figure 2.7.

| ACTIVITY SAMPLING RECORD | | | | | | | | DATE: | | | | |
|---|---|---|---|---|---|---|---|---|---|---|---|---|
| **Activity** | 8.31 | 9.05 | 9.34 | 9.45 | 10.00 | 10.06 | 10.49 | 11.17 | 11.33 | 12.11 | 12.22 | 1.19 |
| SALES FORECASTS | | | | | | | | | | | | |
| RM CALCULATIONS | | | | | | | | | | | | |
| MACHINE SCHEDULES | | | | | | | | | | | | |
| LIAISON | | | | | | | | | | | | |
| PRODUCTION REPORTS | | | | | | | | | | | | |
| TELEPHONE | | | | | | | | | | | | |
| MEETINGS | | | | | | | | | | | | |
| MISCELLANEOUS | | | | | | | | | | | | |
| | | | | | | | | | | | | |
| | | | | | | | | | | | | |
| | | | | | | | | | | | | |

*Figure 2.7* Activity sampling record

**Why random times?** The employee to whom the form applies will be asked to note what he or she is doing at varying times of the day. If the times that he or she does this are regular (say, each hour on the hour), there is a danger that he or she will consciously or unconsciously adjust the activities to record the 'right' activity. The use of random times reduces this possibility and helps to ensure that the sample is representative.

## *Step 4*

A supply of the forms – each one with a different set of times taken from a table of random numbers – is given to the employee, who will be instructed to work as normal, but to tick the activity he or she is engaged in at the times shown on the form.

The employee can be told not to worry too much if the time is missed by a minute or two and not to bother if he or she is away from the workplace for *personal* reasons (meals, visits to the washroom etc.).

If absence from the workplace is say, in order to attend a meeting, he or she should tick the appropriate box or tick 'miscellaneous' if there is no listed and appropriate activity.

**A reminder** It is a good idea to remind the employees that ticking the boxes is under their own control. An honest performance is required but it should be made clear that they are not on trial. It is the work that is being examined, not the people doing it and employees should be very clear on this important point.

## *Step 5*

The employee, or employees, complete their forms day by day and the ticks are totalled for each activity.

Sometimes five or six working days are enough to form a picture of what is going on, but in some cases it is desirable to extend the sampling over a period of five to six weeks. This is to ensure that any cyclical activities are fully covered, e.g. a production planner may spend more time scrutinising sales forecasts during one part of the month than another, so too short a period could give a misleading answer.

Statistically, of course, the larger the sample the more accurate the results will be.

Simple percentages can be worked out when all the data has been collected, e.g.:

| Activity | No. of ticks | Percentage |
|---|---|---|
| Sales forecasts | 850 | 37.5 |
| R.M. calculations | 79 | 3.5 |
| Machine schedules | 102 | 4.5 |
| Liaison | 350 | 15.4 |
| Production reports | 25 | 1.1 |
| Telephone | 350 | 15.4 |
| Meetings | 110 | 4.8 |
| Miscellaneous | 400 | 17.7 |
| **TOTAL** | **2266** | |

## *Step 6*

The final figures can now be examined, discussed with the employee and some conclusions drawn.

There may be some immediate pointers to the cause or background to the problem being addressed. For example, our production planner spends a lot of time on the sales forecasts (37.5 per cent). This is more than a third of his time. Why?

He also spends 15.4 per cent of his time on the telephone – in addition to meetings and liaison work. What are the nature of the phone calls? Are they incoming or outgoing? Do the phone calls arise because of a fault in the system causing foul-ups which need frequent and urgent corrective action?

It is likely that the employee can provide an explanation for real or apparent anomalies – *once the figures are available to him or her*. Experience shows that prior to actually recording what happens, the people doing the work are not always aware of what goes on. They are so accustomed to the situation that it does not strike them as being out of line.

## Some real-life examples

### *A production planner*

In this actual case the production planner was not able to keep up with the work he was allocated.

Instructions to the production side were not being produced on time and the ordering of raw materials was often muddled. This serious problem was at first regarded as one to be solved by additional staff. However, no one could say why workloads had increased. In theory the volume of work should have been much the same as it was a year or so before when there had been no problems.

Activity sampling revealed that the production planner and his staff were spending a lot of time answering queries from the sales force – queries which should have been directed elsewhere. The planning team was good at answering the queries and always wanted to be helpful. The production planner, although he knew that they were doing this work, had not appreciated how much time was being taken up by it. The volume had grown very gradually over the months.

The simple solution was to stop the queries coming and to make sure that the proper department gave the sales force a satisfactory service.

### *A costly maintenance gang*

The labour costs of a manufacturing plant were too high for comfort. Activity sampling was carried out among various operators – many of whom had 'irregular' work – keeping records, checking equipment, opening and closing valves, and the like.

Maintenance was provided by a separate gang and it was found that they too were frequently involved in the various operations. The manager knew that this happened 'from time to time', but had no idea of the actual frequency.

Further sampling revealed that the level of maintenance

needed was less than had been allowed for. The result was a redefining of jobs with maintenance being merged into operations. Some retraining was required, but the result was a smaller workforce and a more effective one.

### *Spotting some bottlenecks*

A clerical section of five people was responsible for processing new business coming in. This involved dealing with an unavoidably complex 'order entry form'. Care was needed over various code numbers, the extraction of statistics and the 'translation' of data into a form which was usable by other departments.

There was a substantial, growing and damaging backlog.

The section supervisor had put forward a plan to solve the backlog problem which involved increasing her staff to fifteen! Management were understandably aghast at this notion and activity sampling of the section was carried out.

This revealed the following.

- Paperwork was passed to and fro among section members. This caused delays as each movement resulted in the paper waiting in a queue.
- Virtually everything done was checked – resulting in more delays.
- Then, everything was checked again by the supervisor, whose desk was a substantial bottleneck.
- Some of the work done would have been better passed to other departments further down the line. There was in fact a lot of time spent referring to these other departments.

The result was that work which could have been done more effectively elsewhere was transferred and the system of checking reduced to a secure but more sensible level.

The routeing of paperwork was changed so that one person carried out a number of functions – in one go – rather than passing the paper to a colleague.

The bottleneck problem was solved with the added bonus that the section was reduced from five people to three as natural wastage occurred over the next twelve months.

Prior to the activity sampling, the actual time spent on checking and the like was not fully appreciated or thought about.

# 7. PARETO – AND RATIOS IN GENERAL

> 'In any series of elements to be controlled a selected small fraction in terms of number of elements almost always accounts for a large fraction in terms of effect.'

So said Vilfredo Pareto, an Italian economist. His statement has come to be known as Pareto's principle – or, more familiarly, the eighty:twenty rule – and holds that if you have a problem it is probably caused by only a small part of whatever it is you are looking at.

Here are some examples.

- High stock-holding costs are likely to be caused by a few items out of many. A retail shop supplying car accessories found that most of the value of its stock was accounted for by a few expensive *and slow-moving* items such as wheels. The value of run-of-the-mill sparking plugs, tins of oil, fan belts and wiper blades was not significant.

  Having discovered this the shop owner cut his costs by arranging a call-off system with suppliers of the expensive items.
- High staff turnover or absenteeism is likely to be largely accounted for only by a section of the workforce.
- Customer complaints and other problems such as slow payment of bills are likely to be restricted to a few customers.

The principle that a few items among many cause the problem has wide applications and can lead you to identify the root of a problem. It can also show where monitoring and control should be concentrated in order to get the best return for time and money.

In a spare parts store, for example, it is probably not worth having elaborate controls on split pins, washers and screws when the bulk of the value is represented by motors, machine tools and diamond-tipped drills.

## When to use the eighty:twenty principle

The principle can be applied whenever there are large 'populations' involved. This includes:

- many branches of the business;
- many customers;
- a wide range of machines;
- a lengthy product list;
- large quantities of paper, e.g. incoming invoices;
- alternative suppliers;
- a fleet of vehicles;
- a team of sales representatives.

It is sometimes obvious which part of the population is causing the problem – but not always. Before taking action on a broad front it is useful to examine such facts as are available, or to set up a recording system, to see if the problem can be isolated. This approach can be especially valuable where there are a number of products sharing production resources. It is likely that most of any losses (or profits) are brought about by a few of them. These need to be identified so that they can be dealt with. Isolating the trouble-makers is more effective than, say, a cost-cutting exercise across the board – which may damage the better products in your range.

## Look for other useful ratios

Pareto, when stating his principle, was pointing to ratios in large 'populations'. However, ratios can also be widely used as an aid to problem solving as they provide some standard information which can be used to measure the size of the tasks to be tackled and, by providing a benchmark, warn of adverse trends.

The following ratios have fairly wide applications and all or some of them could suit your business:

**Activity** hours worked: hours available

**Production** units produced: budgeted units

| | |
|---|---|
| **Sales** | value of sales made: number of calls<br>volume of sales: number of calls |
| **Administration** | incorrect invoices: number received<br>errors: number of transactions |
| **Quality** | rejects: units produced<br>complaints: number of sales |

By maintaining records to provide information of this type, any developing problem area can be identified. If rejects are increasing this can be spotted and, if Pareto's principle is applied, it might be found that the trouble is mostly attributable to one section of the production set-up.

The information gleaned can point the way to the appropriate corrective action, e.g.:

- training or retraining of sales people;
- revision to paperwork;
- adjustments to or replacement of a machine;
- improved supervision in a particular area;
- cutting out a product altogether.

Or, if the ratios reveal an opportunity, benefits could be gained by say:

- putting more sales effort into a particular region;
- increasing production of a product;
- installing another machine.

Hopefully, many of your problems will turn out to be opportunities when you have collected the information.

# 8. JOB EVALUATION

Job evaluation is a fact-finding technique designed to achieve one very important function. It provides a means to assess the relative values of different jobs. This, in turn, enables employers to:

- negotiate rates of pay with employees or their representatives backed up by information to support their case;
- ensure that pay differentials between jobs are fair and reasonable;
- introduce job grading on the basis of an objective assessment rather than some intuitive or subjective thinking.

*Warning:* The results of a job evaluation will only be perfect by sheer chance! It should be recognised that there will be a margin of error and that over subsequent months occasional adjustments may be necessary. However, despite some flaws which may exist in the results, the outcome will be a good deal better than any seat-of-the-pants method for deciding pay scales.

## How does job evaluation work?

It must first be clearly understood that job evaluation concerns, as it suggests, the *job*. The *person* doing the job is not being assessed in any way. This is an important and fundamental point which must be constantly borne in mind throughout any job-evaluation exercise. The relative values of the individuals must be treated separately and additionally.

The valuation process works in the following way.

### *Job attributes*

A standard list of job attributes is drawn up and an evaluation form created. The form could look something like that shown in Figure 2.8.

| Job evaluation form | | Job title: |
|---|---|---|
| ATTRIBUTE | SCORE | EXPLANATION (IF REQUIRED) |
| Responsibility for people<br>Responsibility for money<br>Responsibility for machinery<br>Degree of concentration<br>Cost impact of errors<br>Time span of decisions<br>Physical demands<br>Basic qualifications<br>Training and experience<br>Social skills (internal)<br>Social skills (external) | | |
| TOTAL SCORE | | |

*Figure 2.8* Job evaluation form

Attributes can be selected according to the general nature of the jobs being evaluated. Office jobs may well demand a different selection from factory floor jobs and service industry companies will require something different from manufacturers.

Care is needed when defining what is inherent in an attribute and a good measure of common sense must be applied when you reach the stage of placing a score against them (see below).

Look at the attributes listed on the form:

**Responsibility for people**

This is normally a straightforward question. If a job involves supervision of ten clerks then it must be more demanding than one which involves only five clerks.

**Responsibility for money**

This usually means cash or negotiable securities, i.e. something which can be stolen or misapplied. The implication in the attribute is the amount of care needed to guard against loss.

**Responsibility for machinery**
Again, this is normally straightforward. The value of the machinery and the care required are to be assessed. The pilot of a wide-body jet has more to look after than the pilot of a two-seater.

**Degree of concentration**
This refers to the mental effort required by the job. An example is computer programming which demands *substantial* concentration, as do teaching, language interpretation and aspects of legal work.

**Cost impact of errors**
This attribute may, in some jobs, be clearly linked to responsibility for money and machinery – but not always. Design engineering, architecture, production planning and sales forecasting are all examples of jobs which can result in major costs if errors are made, although direct responsibility for assets may be limited.

**Time span of decisions**
Corporate planning may involve looking ahead for five, ten or even twenty years. A mistake now could be devastating in, say two to three years' time. Generally speaking, the further ahead the time when a decision taken now will have its impact, the greater is the value of the job. This is often a case of drawing a distinction between tactical jobs and strategic jobs.

**Physical demands**
This attribute concerns factors such as noise, heat and dirt to be endured and the sheer physical effort required.

**Basic qualifications**
These are the essential minimum qualifications required for the job. A law degree may be required to handle certain types of insurance claims, or a qualification in chemistry may be necessary for a job in food technology or food manufacture.

Most often the basic qualification is obvious (e.g. doctors, architects, accountants and engineers), but not always.

**Training and experience**
This is frequently the training and experience required *after* obtaining a basic qualification and without which the job cannot be effectively done. This attribute often reflects the difference between education and training.

**Social skills (internal and external)**
Some jobs demand more social skills than others. Contacts with customers and visitors, handling complaints and chasing up debtors all require a high degree of sensitivity to others and the ability to work diplomatically.

Internal contacts can also demand high degrees of skill, for example in personnel work and counselling. Social skills include, for example, a knowledge of courteous behaviour (which varies from country to country) and a job involving dealings with people from other countries can be very demanding in this respect.

## *Evaluation team*

Having selected the appropriate list of attributes an 'evaluation team' is required. The role of the team will be to assess each job being evaluated and to award a points score to each attribute of each job. A range of one to ten can be used.

Four people is a suitable number with which to form a team. Fewer than four reduces the amount of knowledge present to a level which is probably too low, while a larger team will probably take an unnecessarily long time to reach its conclusions.

As an example of what sort of people should comprise the team the following evaluated a series of office jobs:

- the computer department manager;
- a clerk/typist;
- an organisation and methods analyst;
- an accounts department section supervisor.

In reserve were a secretary and a personal assistant.

In another case where factory jobs were under consideration the team was made up of:

- a chemical engineer;
- chief storekeeper;
- a fitter;
- the personnel manager.

**Who should be in the team?**
The essential requirements for team membership are:

- plenty of common sense;
- a good knowledge of the company and its activities;
- regular contact with the grass-roots employees.

The last of these requirements often excludes very senior people and, since credibility is an essential requirement of the results of job evaluation, it is better seen as the work of 'ordinary' employees rather than a boardroom sub-committee. (*Note:* When points are being awarded for the job done by any member of the team, that member should be temporarily replaced by a substitute. Justice must be seen to be done.)

## *The briefing*

The team, once formed and briefed, can start its work. The briefing should include the following points.

- A reminder that it is *the job* which is being assessed and not the people doing it or those who hold the jobs being assessed. Team members must put out of their minds any views they may have of the capabilities or quality of individuals they know – and be careful not to be influenced by personal likes and dislikes.
- Each of the attributes of each job should be fully discussed by the team and, if there is any clear doubt or disagreement, they should seek more information about the job in question.

## *Awarding the points*

This to some extent will be arbitrary, but to reduce the possibility of unfairness, a set of standards should be used. This amounts to a series of benchmarks such as the following.

- *Responsibility for people:*
  Direct charge of five people = five points
- *Responsibility for money:*
  cashier = ten points
- *Physical demands:*
  lorry driver = four points
  lathe operator = two points
- *Social skills:*
  receptionist = eight points
  salesperson = ten points
  computer analyst = four points

The team will relate the attributes they are considering to the list of standards given and ask the question, 'Does this job rate higher, lower or the same?' (*Note:* It is sometimes found during the course of the evaluation that the standards are wrong. If this is the case, there should be no hesitation in changing them and starting again. Job evaluation is too important an activity to be carried out in a hurry or without proper care being taken.)

The team should have, and refer to, up-to-date job descriptions and, if required, should ask questions of one or more people doing the job being studied to ensure that they have a proper understanding of it. Of course, heads of departments can be questioned about the jobs of their staff, but answers from this quarter should be treated with caution. Experience shows that managers do not always have a full and accurate knowledge of what their staff have to do.

The points for each attribute of each job are entered on the appropriate form and then totalled. This, however, is not the end of the exercise.

## *The long stop*

As an aid to ensuring that justice is seen to be done it is wise to have the results of the team's work examined by appropriate managers and supervisors. Their views, if contrary, should be passed back to the team for consideration and a rethink. The team may well amend the scores for one or more jobs as a result of the rethink, but they may not.

An important rule to be followed is that the decision of the team should be final.

If this rule is not followed, then some unbalanced ratings can be given. In one company the managing director insisted on making the final decision himself. This resulted in the job of secretary to the MD being rated higher than any of the departmental manager jobs. This was because he awarded maximum points for the following.

- Responsibility for money. The MD's secretary kept a stock of travellers cheques for him to use.
- Social skills. It was argued that if the MD's secretary was rude to say, the MD of a major customer company, the result could be disastrous.
- Responsibility for people. The MD reckoned that his secretary was senior to *all* non-executive people in the company. This gave her a 'staff' of about 200!

Such mistakes must also be avoided by the team. A high award for social skills should not be given on the possible consequences of being rude to someone. It should be assumed that not being rude can be taken for granted, whereas skilful diplomacy may not.

Similarly, responsibility for people is not a reflection of hierarchical status, but the actual number of people who report direct to the holder of the job being assessed. The job title, possession of a company car and reserved parking space (for instance) are not relevant to the job attributes which command points.

## *What happens next?*

Once the team has completed their work, the job evaluation as such is completed. The result is a fund of information about the jobs and their relative 'values'.

This information can now be used by management (frequently on the personnel side) to tackle such problems as pay scales and grading.

The information can be used to negotiate with unions or other employee representatives, or perhaps to restructure the company pay scheme for future years. There will, of course, be other information thrown into the melting pot – not least the going rate for a job in the market. The going rates will not negate the job-evaluation results which provide a set of *relative* values.

# 9. MARKET RESEARCH

Despite the many books written on the subject, the attention it receives in the business press and its prominence in management training, market research is still neglected, particularly by small to medium-sized business. Anecdotal evidence suggests that the neglect may be due to the following:

- a lack of appreciation of the importance of a business being market-driven as opposed to being product-driven;
- a belief that market research must of necessity be expensive and time-consuming;
- lack of awareness of some relatively simple ways to gather market information;
- 'We are too busy to spare people for market research.'

and, most dangerous of all, 'We know what our customers want' or 'Sales are good, we have nothing to worry about'.

The nature of the market for your product or service – and what that market *wants* – will be a crucial factor in determining your future performance. However well designed and skilfully made your product may be, it will only sell if:

- there is a demand for it. 'Demand' means a sufficient number of people who not only want to buy your product but can also afford the price you are asking. For example, millions of people would like to buy a Rolls-Royce – but few can afford one
- there is no substitute product offered at a lower price which, even if inferior to yours, is preferred by the market.

Market research involves finding out what the market is really like, where genuine customers are located, how much they will pay, and the quality standards they require. You may find that your quality standards (and price) will suit only a small segment of the market and, if so, you need to know what and where this segment is. You also need to know to what extent competitors are already active in this segment.

Above all you need to make a stab at estimating the *future* needs of the market. For example:

- changes in population numbers will affect demand;
- demographic shifts (e.g. more or fewer teenagers) will influence what people want;
- rising or falling living standards can determine whether or not certain products or services will do well. This factor becomes particularly apparent whenever there is a recession. Luxury goods and leisure activities tend to suffer first and most markedly.

Market research can help you to decide which way to go and, if it is properly done and the results carefully analysed, can both help to avoid disasters and expose opportunities.

## What problems can be tackled by market research?

There are many (and serious) problems which can face a business for which up-to-date information from the market may be needed. They include:

- a falling share of the market;
- static sales in a growing market;
- whether or not to modify a product or service;
- whether or not to discontinue a product or service;
- whether or not to develop and launch a new product;
- deciding the optimum product mix;
- uncertainty about the value of advertising or other promotional methods;
- lack of information about the potential size of a market or the likely demand for a product or service;
- uncertainty about price levels;
- whether or not to invest more money in the sales effort, e.g. by increasing the sales force;
- whether or not to move into new geographical areas.

All these problems relate to (a) what the customers want and (b) the future. This means that fundamental to solving the problem is the obtaining of data which at least gives a strong indication of what the market wants now and will want in the future.

## How to go about obtaining the data

There are five ways in which information can be collected:

- researching published reports;
- conducting interviews;
- postal surveys;
- telephone surveys;
- panel interviews.

These methods, which can be approached in a variety of ways, can also be used to obtain information on marketing methods (market*ing* research), e.g. by assessing the impact of advertising.

The various options for obtaining the information required must be considered carefully in order to select those which are appropriate to your particular business. Care must also be taken to recognise, and make maximum use of, cheap and easy ways which may be open to you to collect the facts. We will now look at the five basic methods.

### *Researching published reports*

A large amount of information is available from:

- government publications;
- newspaper surveys;
- trade associations;
- local authorities.

An example of how this information can be used comes from the insurance industry. A company had devised a new insurance service aimed, primarily, at ship agents. These potential customers, providing services to ship owners, could be found in ports around the world. The company, wishing to concentrate its initial efforts on the most promising countries (and ports) in Europe, sought information on the number of ship agents operating in them.

This apparently difficult task was readily accomplished by obtaining (often from port authorities) copies of the port handbooks and ship agent association handbooks. These documents listed all the ship agents, port by port, giving details of their addresses, which shipping lines they acted for and listing their main activities.

Subsequent analysis of this information resulted in the selection and prioritisation of target areas. The sales force concentrated on these areas and rapidly established a sizeable customer base. Once this was achieved, efforts were concentrated on some lower-level targets. It was also noteworthy that no time and money were wasted on areas with little to offer.

**Local information**

Businesses which concentrate their efforts in one area or are setting their sights on sales in, say, one large town, can make a good start by examining local trade directories, the *Thomson Directory* and *Yellow Pages*. From such sources an indication will be gained of the number of potential sources of business. Imagine, for instance, a company intending to sell office machinery in a given area. The potential size of the market could be assessed by counting the number of likely users such as:

building societies;<br>
solicitors;<br>
accountants;<br>
insurance brokers;<br>
insurance companies;<br>
local government offices;<br>
company head or branch offices;<br>
estate agents.

At the same time the size of the competition can be checked by seeing – in the same directories – who offers the same products.

Checking through advertisements in newspapers can also assist in picking out the potential customers – and the competition.

**Looking wider**

Government and other survey reports detailing the nature of populations, e.g. by age distribution and income groups, are all useful. Similarly, data is also available showing how many people have washing machines, video players and other goods. If your product or service is in any way related to such factors, the figures contained in these surveys can give you clues to future prospects.

**Conducting interviews**

There are companies which provide interviewing services, for example, sending their interviewers into the streets with clipboards and questionnaires. These may suit your purpose and pocket, but you may also be able to do it yourself using your own sales force or other employees.

Much can be done by giving each sales person, or whoever may be in contact with customers, one or two specific questions to ask the customers.

If, say, it is desired to know the likely demand for a new form of packaging or whether or not customers would be willing to pay for an extension to the services already on offer, an appropriate question can be put to them when the sales representative calls. Even if only a percentage of customers are questioned, the answers could be representative of the market as a whole. (*Note:* It is important to put the questions in a neutral way so as not to 'lead the witness' and to avoid a bias creeping in.)

**Postal surveys**

This method of obtaining information tends to be slow, but it is relatively inexpensive.

The usual approach is by means of a questionnaire – which must be designed with care to avoid bias and to obtain the information that is really needed. Three points are crucial to the postal questionnaire method.

- The questions must be clear, unambiguous, only using words that are in everyday use. For example, 'Does the machine react favourably to extremes of ambient temperature?' is less likely to be understood than, 'Do temperature changes cause any problems?' or 'Does the machine work well in both hot and cold weather?'

  Words which have widely differing meanings for different people should also be avoided. For example, words like good, acceptable, nice and pleasing are too vague to be relied on.

- Avoid open-ended *answers*. These are very difficult to analyse and can be avoided by using multiple-choice questions, e.g. 'What do you think is the best feature of our product?' would be better expressed, 'Which of these features do you rate as most important to you –
  Style □ Colour □ Portability □ ?'
- The questionnaire must be easy to complete and should require as little effort as possible on the part of the informant. Hard work (including puzzling it out) will positively discourage replies – as will the lack of pre-paid postage to return the questionnaire.

**Telephone surveys**

Using the telephone to obtain information is relatively easy to organise and less costly than visiting people to talk to them face to face. It is also speedy, in that a dozen or more successful calls can be made in a day by one person.

There will also be a number of unsuccessful calls which reflect the disadvantages in the method, namely:

- some people respond badly to telephone enquiries which they regard as an unwarranted intrusion on their lives;
- calls may be received at an inconvenient time;
- the wrong person may be asked for or may by chance take the call.

Notwithstanding these problems, the telephone survey is used with success particularly in the commercial and industrial world.

**Panel interviews**

Panels are most frequently used for consumer research on products such as washing powder, foods and other consumables.

A group of consumers (100 or more will probably be needed to obtain a representative sample) are provided with 'diaries' in which they record purchases and the TV advertisements and other promotional influences which prompted their actions.

The buying pattern record which results gives an indication

of brand loyalty and the effects of promotional schemes. The relative effectiveness of different forms of advertising, free samples, money-off coupons and the like can then be assessed.

A variation on this theme is to invite (with the incentive of paid expenses and refreshments) a number of people to a meeting. They are asked to fill in a questionnaire on their purchasing habits, preferences and perception of the product.

Participants are then shown an advertisement designed for TV and after, say, a coffee break to let it sink in, they are given the same questionnaire to complete. Any changes in the answers given indicate the degree of influence that the advertisement has had.

Questions can then be asked about the panel members' views of the advertisement itself. This can produce some fascinating results. . .

For example, a panel member, commenting on a TV advertisement for product X already in use for some months expressed her loathing of it. She hated the jingle and the way in which the message was put over.

When asked which product she actually used she declared 'Oh, X of course!' She had never considered any other product despite her dislike of the advertisement.

Such reactions not only say something about the intrinsic qualities of the advertisement, but can suggest that there is some other reason why the consumer buys the product. Finding out what this is can be extremely valuable and point the way to a profitable change in marketing method.

# 10. PILOT TRIALS

Products for the retail market are commonly 'test-marketed' to assess consumer reaction before a commitment to a full production and marketing effort.

This action is taken to reveal any problems in distribution, point-of-sale presentation, packaging and the like, in addition to any unforeseen customer complaints or adverse reaction to the product itself. Test-marketing is probably the first thing to spring to mind when 'pilot trials' are mentioned, but there are many other possible applications of them.

## When to carry out a pilot trial

The following characteristics indicate a situation in which a pilot trial could be used.

- There is significant uncertainty that the idea will work out in practice, often in spite of logic which says that it should.
- The idea involves considerable cost in terms of cash or other resources and the element of risk to the business is significant.
- Proceeding with the idea, even if not particularly expensive in money terms, will have a disruptive effect on the business, e.g. wide staff retraining, relocation of people or assets, or interruptions to work or production.

These characteristics can be found in many non-marketing situations such as:

- computerisation of clerical activities;
- introducing a payment-by-results scheme;
- reducing the frequency of product testing.

These are all situations in which something sounds like a good idea, but if it goes wrong the potential losses could be enormous. Clearly it makes sense to try it out on a small scale in order to see what happens. The pilot trial should be set up with great care to ensure that it is truly representative of the full-scale situation and the following additional precautions taken.

- Full communication should be made to all concerned to avoid reactions such as 'Here's another bloody silly idea *they* have dreamed up' or 'I've no idea what this is all about so I shall ignore it'.
- A careful *and planned* monitoring system must be installed to ensure that the information gained is accurate and objective. The emotional reactions of individuals are likely to be misleading.
- A small team of qualified people should be appointed to evaluate the results – formally. This team, which should ideally include at least one disinterested person, will help to avoid the dangers of too quick an assessment or one which is based on prejudice or gut-feel.
- Any problems which are revealed should be treated as obstacles to be overcome and not reasons to abandon the trial. The team can help to ensure that a potentially good idea does not get rejected as soon as the first difficulty is encountered.

## *A case in point*

A British company had seven small subsidiaries all doing the same job, but with customers in different parts of the world.

The work was characterised by a lot of paperwork – mainly voluminous correspondence with the customers, backed up by reports and other documents. A total of around 50 000 active files were in use by the seven subsidiaries at any one time, plus a similar quantity stored in the archives and which could 'come alive' again.

The problems presented by this situation were:

- very large and expensive storage areas in the company offices;
- problems in keeping track of files, with missing files a constant headache;
- the risk that in the event of a fire or other disaster resulting in loss of the files, the business could be brought to a grinding halt;

- reading the files (e.g. when a new piece of correspondence arrived) was time-consuming and clerical output was low;
- a small army of filing clerks were required to move the files around the offices and to look after the archival items. These staff were costly *and* difficult to recruit. Turnover was high and training the newcomers was another ongoing job;
- selecting the correct file for poorly identified incoming mail was often difficult and consumed much of the time of the more experienced staff.

**The potential solution**

After much agonising it was decided that a 'live-file' microfilm system (using a fiche which could be updated) would solve many, if not all, of the problems.

By no means everyone was in favour of this idea and the objections included the following.

- Considerable costs would be involved in purchasing a camera and film-processor, microfilm readers and sundry other bits of kit. It was pointed out that every clerk would need his or her own reader.
- Every member of staff would have to be trained in the use of the equipment.
- Staff accustomed to dealing with paper for many years would find it difficult to switch to reading from a screen. It was also suggested that constant use of the screens could cause eye-strain and headaches for the staff.
- A special team would have to be trained from scratch to use the camera and processing equipment – the latter needing a water supply.

Some of the doubters based their argument on the simple, if unsupported, statement that 'It just will not work'.

If only for the reason that no other solutions to the paperwork problems had emerged, it was decided to run a pilot trial (using rented equipment) in one of the subsidiaries.

The result was clear proof that the microfilm system would do the trick. Space saving rapidly became apparent and security against fire was dramatically illustrated when a fire actually broke out. Some paper files were destroyed (by water), but they had been microfilmed. The films, stored in duplicate in separate places, were still intact and business could be continued without a break.

It was also found that training was less of a burden than had been feared and the great majority of the people involved adapted readily to the system. In due course all the subsidiaries were added to the system and substantial savings were made. In addition to the release of some 3000ft$^2$ of prime office space (plus basement space), the number of filing clerks was reduced. Sixteen out of twenty jobs disappeared over the months through natural wastage.

## Simulation – a variation on a theme

Simulating a situation as a means to test what would happen given various alternative actions or circumstances is becoming commonplace. Normally these simulations are based on a complicated computer programme and quite a lot of high-tech hardware. Treasury forecasts and even weather forecasts are examples of the simulation technique in use.

Perhaps because the use of computers makes it all sound expensive and complicated, few businesses apart from really big ones seem to use simulation. They will nevertheless have 'What if?' problems to solve from time to time which are not suitable for spread-sheets or other standard computer packages. The cost of designing and writing the computer software can be avoided by a 'pencil and paper' approach which also gets results – which are sometimes more reliable.

### *The pencil and paper method*

The method is best illustrated by a real-life example taken from a manufacturing company. The company manufactured plastic granules which were used by customers for making end-products such as housewares, toys, radio casings and different forms of packaging.

There was one basic material produced – but in a number of

grades. Each grade could be coloured, according to customers' requirements, in one of a very wide range of colours.

Orders arrived in a fairly random fashion and since colour requirements varied from order to order, only the basic materials could be made for stock. This stock was stored in hoppers which formed part of the production line. Storage in any other way was not possible for a number of reasons, including the necessity to protect the product from dust and other contaminants.

The problem to be solved concerned the use of the hoppers. However hard the factory management tried they could never make optimum use of them. If a customer wanted grade A product the chances were that the hoppers contained anything but grade A. Some hoppers would be only part filled with product for which there was no immediate demand, but which effectively blocked the production of product which *was* in demand.

Delays in meeting customer demand occurred (to the fury of the sales staff) and at any given time much of the hopper capacity was idle.

Various suggestions were made for solving the problem, including installing more hoppers. These were expensive alternatives and there was little room in the factory to place additional equipment. It was decided to simulate the factory's operation to see if a solution would emerge.

**What happened?**

All the orders received over the previous six months were collected together. The exact situation in the factory on a day six months before was dug out from the records and put down on paper. This provided a 'status report' showing the contents of the hoppers, work in progress, machinery undergoing maintenance and so on.

A team was then formed comprising the senior foreman, the production engineer, a control clerk and one or two other people involved in day-to-day operations.

Two 'umpires' were selected – one an accountant to calculate run costs and the other an engineer with a detailed knowledge of the way the factory worked.

The simulation started with the team being given the 'status report'. They were allowed time to study it and were then issued with a customer's order – followed by others in the exact sequence in which they had arrived in real life.

Over the next two to three hours the team continued to receive orders and were presented with details of machine failures, staff shortages and other variable factors – all taken from records from the past. The team made decisions minute by minute of what to manufacture, how to use the hoppers and other equipment – in short, they simulated the operation of the factory.

The umpires were there to ensure 'fair play' and also observed the results of the decisions made.

**What was discovered?**

The effect of compressing six months into a few hours, coupled with everyone present being able to see what was going on in all parts of the factory at the same time yielded valuable information.

Among other things the team were able to see:

- aspects requiring greater co-ordination of the activities of engineers and other decision-takers;
- ways in which hoppers could be put to better use;
- the need for changes to the system for recording and notifying orders in the pipeline, production failures, maintenance needs and the like.

Much useful information was gained and after some time spent analysing it, the simulation was repeated under new operating rules resulting from the experience of the first simulation.

The result was a number of real-life changes which reduced operating costs and improved customer service. No money had to be spent on additional hoppers.

The main advantage of simulation, apart from its low cost, is the fact that the brief time-span makes it possible to see the effects (good or bad) of decisions. In real life the span of time is much greater, and cause and effect are not so obvious, so bad practices cannot be seen as such and are persisted with.

# Part 3

# How to Analyse the Information You've Collected

In many cases the collection of the information involves a degree of analysis. The information may therefore be partly or fully digested and the required decision to solve the problem may be fairly obvious.

It is also not infrequently found that the information gained results in a change to the perceived problem. In the case of the factory simulation described in Part 2.10, above, many people defined the problem as one of a shortage of hopper capacity. The information gained from the simulation showed that the problem was in fact one of co-ordination and control.

Assuming, however, that the original problem definition was correct, ways and means of analysing the information collected are required. This is, as often as not, a question of how it is presented.

# 1. PRESENTING THE INFORMATION

Skilful presentation of the data collected will:

- make it possible to see the wood and not just the trees;
- help to present a true impression of what the information means.

A graph, for example, will meet these needs – or will it? Take a look at the graph in Figure 3.1 (on page 77), which suggests a substantial increase in sales. This could lead to some optimistic conclusions – even complacent ones – and appropriate decisions then may be taken.

Now look at Figure 3.2. The sales figures are exactly the same, but now appear to be much less favourable. They are still on the increase but not so dramatically. The reason is that in Figure 3.1 the vertical axis does not start at zero while in Figure 3.2 it does.

In both cases the percentage rise in sales and the tonnage differences over the period are identical, yet, at first glance, Figure 3.1 looks wonderful while Figure 3.2 is just good.

Graphs are, therefore, a first-class medium for self-delusion (or deluding others), unless properly used. Proper use means putting in the full scale on the axes and avoiding the worst sin of all – no scale at all!

## Making sense of the figures

A well-designed graph can make sense of a welter of figures. Consider, for example, information relating to sales results and expenditure on promotion. The figures may look like this:

| | **Sales £s** | **Advertising £s** |
|---|---|---|
| JAN. 1990 | 2.6 Million | 11 000 |
| FEB. | 3.0 Million | 10 000 |
| MAR. | 2.8 Million | – |
| APR. | 2.4 Million | 5 000 |
| MAY. | 2.4 Million | 5 000 |
| JUN. | 2.4 Million | 5 000 |
| JUL. | 2.4 Million | 10 000 |
| AUG. | 2.8 Million | – |
| SEP. | 2.4 Million | 10 000 |
| OCT. | 1.8 Million | 5 000 |
| NOV. | 2.0 Million | 5 000 |
| DEC. | 1.6 Million | – |
| JAN. 1991 | 1.4 Million | 10 000 |
| FEB. | 1.8 Million | 5 000 |
| MAR. | 2.2 Million | 5 000 |

The figures suggest that there is no correlation between the amount spent on advertising and the level of sales. Although sales in February 1990 were high when a lot of money was spent on advertising, they were almost as good in March 1990 when there was no advertising at all.

Equally puzzling is the fact that in August when no money was spent sales rose *above* the July figure when a large sum was spent. To add to the puzzle we see that sales in January 1991 were at their lowest point. January 1991 was a month in which advertising expenditure was higher than for any of the three preceding months.

Now look at the same figures in graph form in Figure 3.3 (on page 78). It will be seen that the line of the sales figures follows the advertising line in terms of ups and downs, but with a lag of one to two months. In other words, the effect of the advertising is positive but delayed.

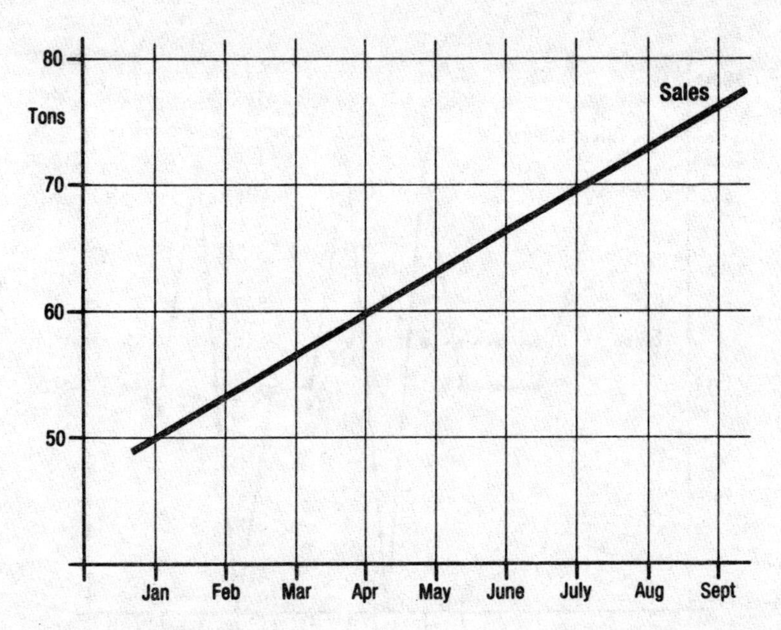


*Figure 3.1* Sales graph 1

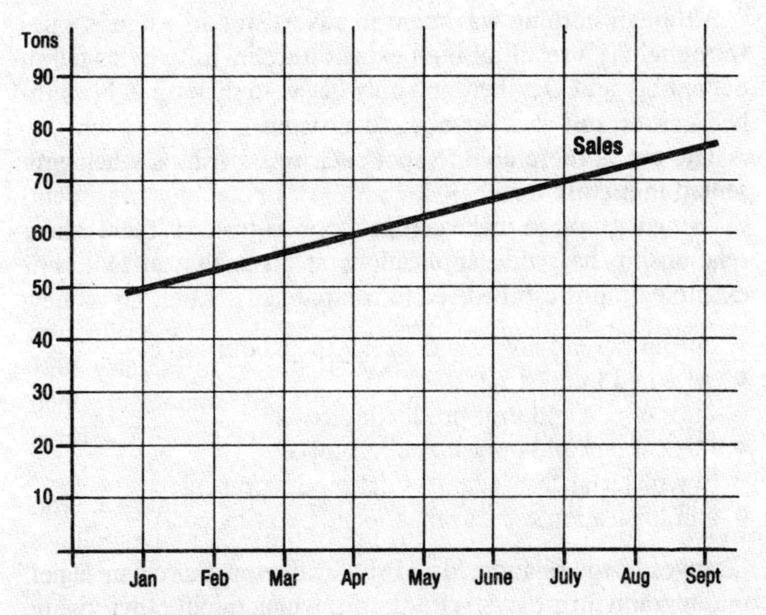


*Figure 3.2* Sales graph 2

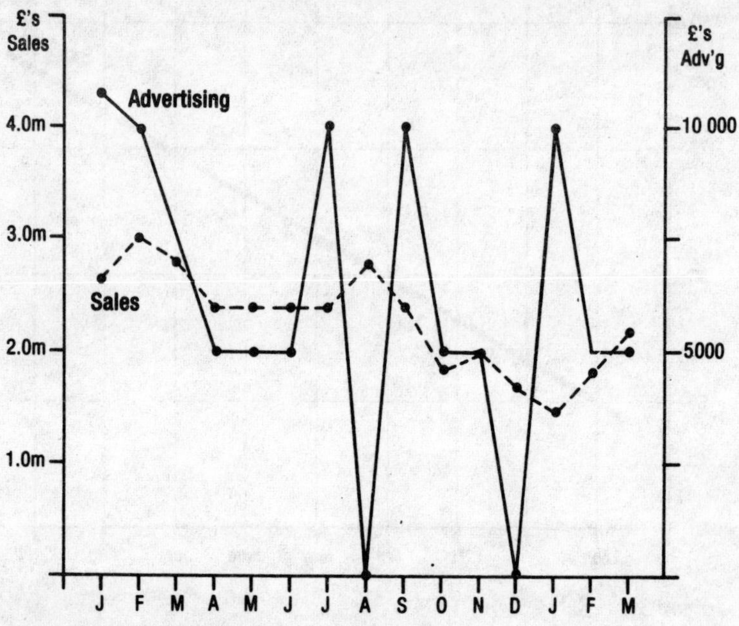


*Figure 3.3* Sales graph 3

Although nothing was spent in advertising in August, sales were high as a result of high expenditure in July. Sales fell in September and October, and only began to pick up in November – as a result of September advertising.

The eye is more able to spot such relationships when presented in picture form.

Using a graph to make comparisons or to see if there is any relationship has wide applications as an analytical tool. For example graphs can be used to compare:

- output per employee and size of the labour force;
- sales and interest rates;
- rates of pay and unit production costs;
- rates of pay and output per employee;
- raw material costs against total production costs;
- administration costs against total operating costs.

Changes in the relationship of such values as these can, when put in graph form, make clear trends which might otherwise be difficult to spot.

Another way to make things clearer is to use a horizontal or vertical bar chart.

## Bar charts

There are a number of kinds of bar chart which can be used – some more visually and analytically effective than others.

They can be in either horizontal or vertical form – the horizontal usually being used to compare quantities and the vertical to represent a 'time-series' (see pages 80–82).

Figure 3.4 shows a horizontal bar chart and Figure 3.5 a vertical chart.

Such charts can be varied to draw attention to aspects of importance by means of colouring or by using lines to enhance comparisons. An example of this is shown in Figure 3.6.

Another variation which aids comparison is a bar chart with values in ascending or descending order. An example of this is shown in Figure 3.7.

Yet another comparison can be made by placing the bars above or below a line representing a key value. This method is shown in Figure 3.8.

### *Multiple comparisons with a bar chart*

Bars can be sub-divided to enable more than one overall comparison to be made. In this way the relative merits of, say, different products can be compared together with, perhaps, the constituent costs of those products. This arrangement is illustrated in Figure 3.9 (on page 82).

Setting out the information in this form not only makes it easier to assimilate, but the breakdown also draws attention to possible solutions to problems. Suppose, for example, that product X was making a loss. The high labour-cost content of the overall product cost may have been accepted as 'normal' – until the comparison with the labour costs of the other products was made. Is labour cost out of control? Can anything be learned from the other products and the reason for their lower labour costs?

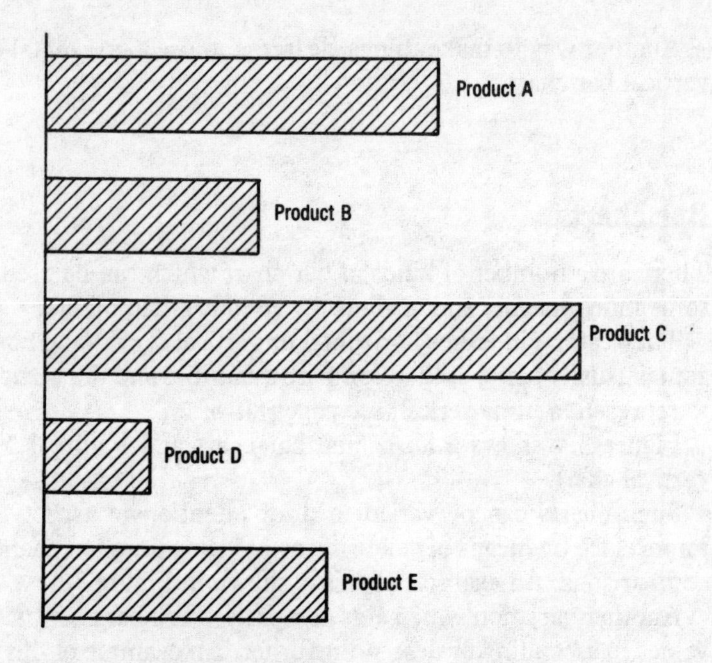


*Figure 3.4* A horizontal bar chart

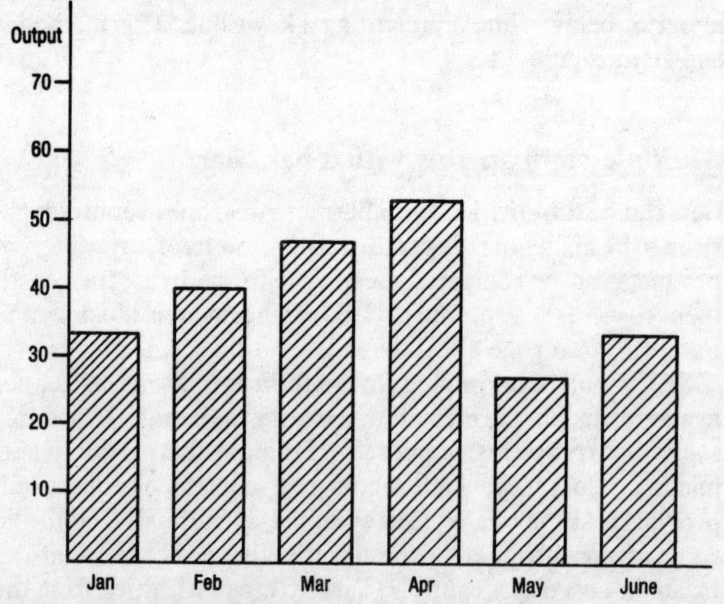


*Figure 3.5* A vertical bar chart

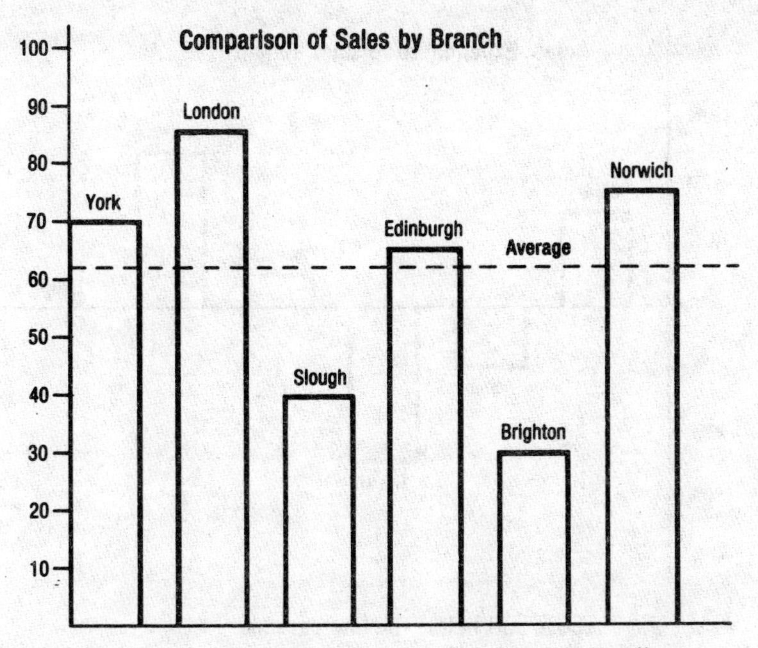


*Figure 3.6* Enhancing a comparison by using an average line

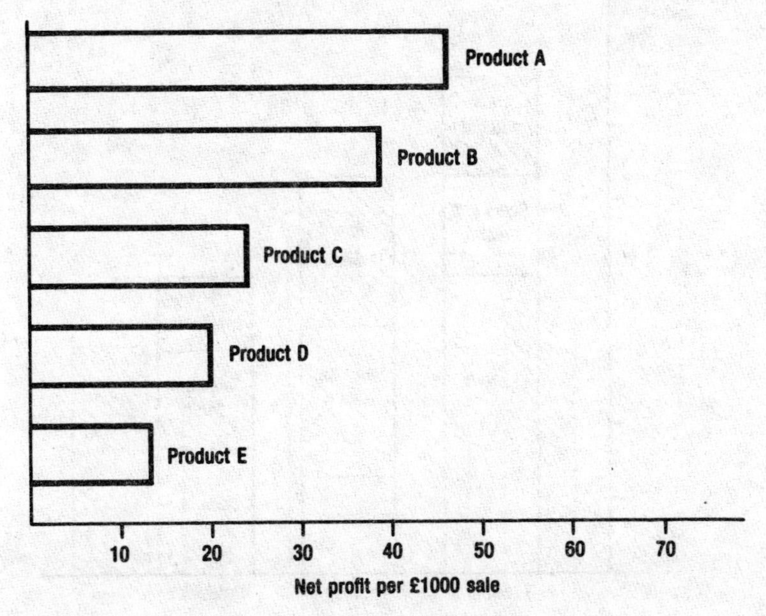


*Figure 3.7* Ranking to enhance comparisons

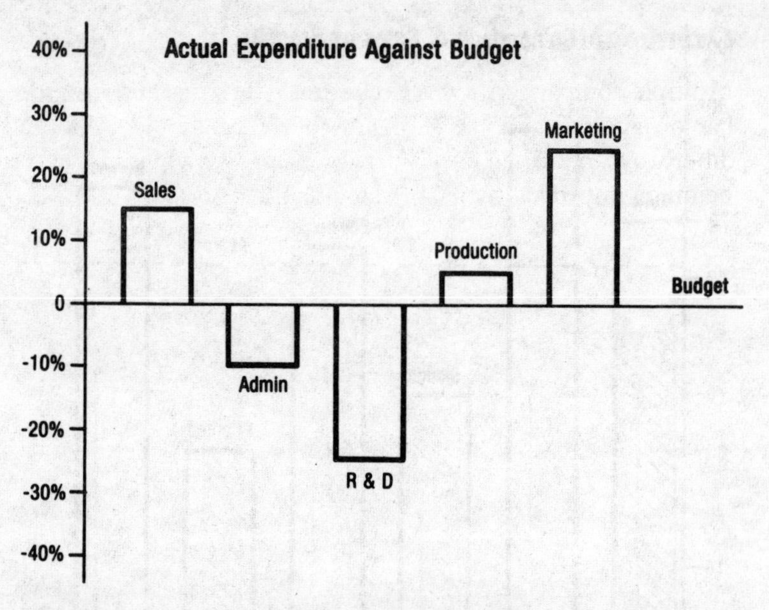


*Figure 3.8* Above and below the line bar chart

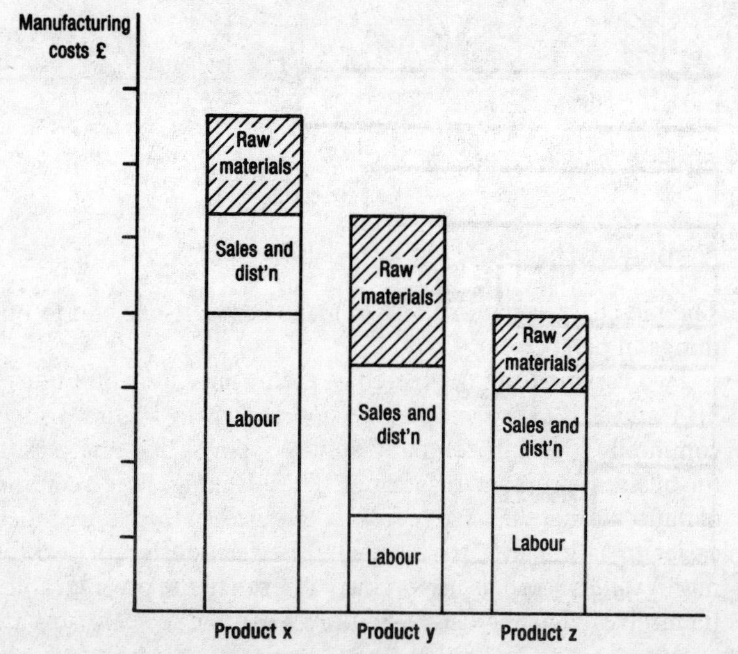


*Figure 3.9* Making multiple comparisons

## *Overlapping bars*

Multiple comparisons can also be made by superimposing one bar on another. Figure 3.10 provides an example. This and other ways to put the facts and figures into a pictorial form can be much improved by using colours and shading.

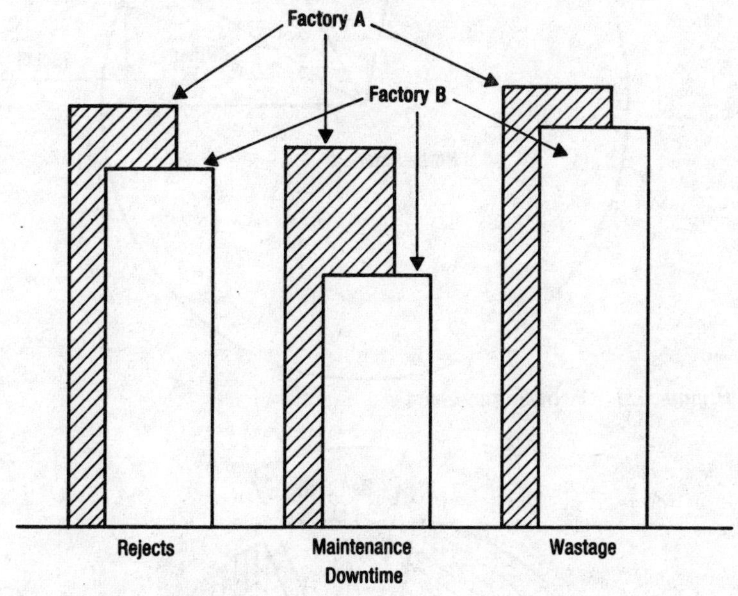


*Figure 3.10* Superimposing the bars

# A slice of the pie

The pie-chart is another way to make comparisons and to put things in perspective.

Two variations on the pie-chart theme are shown in Figures 3.11 and 3.12. The simpler version shown in Figure 3.11 is commonly found in company annual reports, and analyses in the business press and magazines. The advantage over a column of figures is that the relative sizes of the slices of the pie are much easier to assimilate. It is normally the relationship of two (or more) values which is important, rather than the precise values themselves. The pie-chart will draw attention to such facts as:

- administrative costs are nearly as high as production costs;

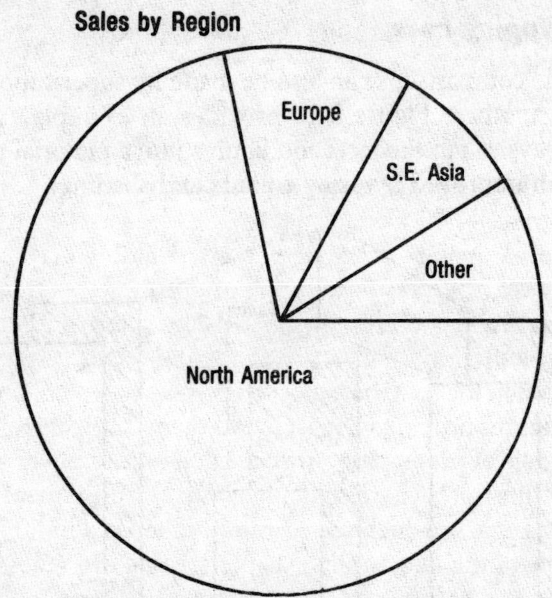


*Figure 3.11* A basic pie-chart

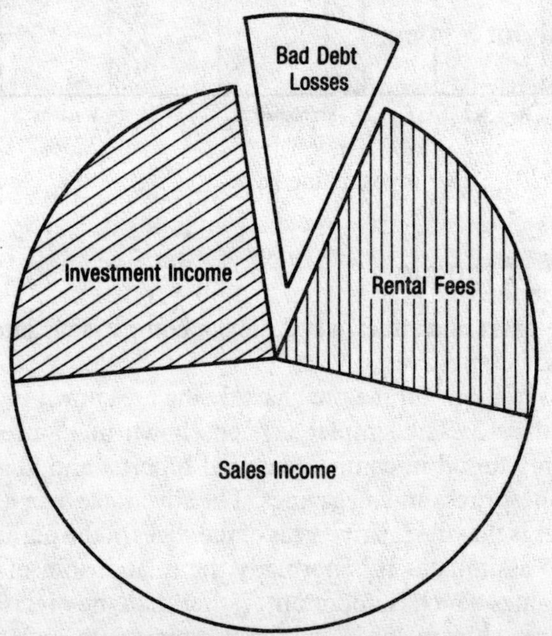


*Figure 3.12* Highlighting a significant figure by taking a slice from the pie

- more than half of earnings are from one, possibly vulnerable, product;
- research and development expenditure is less than the amount spent on entertainment, or whatever.

This method of analysis can have a valuable spin-off if you are trying to sell an idea or otherwise influence people. For example, a major British company makes a report to its employees every year. The report provides facts and figures on what percentage of revenue has been spent on purchases, property and, importantly, dividends and wages. The company found that in the past the majority of employees were unaffected by the figures provided – most found them confusing or boring. A new style of presentation was decided on and pie-charts were used to illustrate where the money went. Subsequent surveys showed a marked increase in the number of employees who took note of the figures and much increased awareness of their meaning.

## *Taking out a slice*

The pie-chart shown in Figure 3.12 has a slice detached from the main body of the pie. This is a useful device for drawing attention to a value which needs something to be done about it.

If, as in Figure 3.12, a bad debts figure needs to be put further into perspective, another pie-chart might be prepared showing profit as one of its slices. If this second pie-chart is placed alongside the first – or if prepared on a transparent sheet laid over the first – the effect of bad debts on profit will be painfully obvious.

# 2. THE PAY-OFF MATRIX

Imagine a company which has designed a new product for the leisure market. We will call that product the Wongo.

The Wongo, like the skate-board and the hula-hoop before it, could be all the rage and sell in enormous quantities. It could, alternatively, be a complete flop.

The company has little to go on from market research since the Wongo has no similar predecessors and all that is available is a collection of widely varying gut-feel reactions.

The only positive information available comes from within the company and is as follows:

- the factory could not operate effectively if less than 400 Wongos are produced each day;
- the maximum possible output is 1000 Wongos per day;
- any Wongos not sold will cost £10 each to hold in stock.

It is also believed that the Wongos can be sold at a price which will yield £20 contribution each.

Clearly this is a risky situation. In particular, since the demand from the market (at the price set) is unknown, the problem is how many Wongos to make at any one time.

The pessimists will propose the minimum possible quantity (400) and the optimists might go for the maximum quantity (1000).

## Maximin and maximax

These are not in fact a pair of comedians, but the names given to two 'decision rules' which can be applied in situations of uncertainty.

Under the maximin rule the person making the decision chooses the alternative which maximises the minimum pay-off. This is the pessimist's approach.

The optimist will seek the maximax alternative and chooses the alternative which will result in maximising the maximum pay-off.

We can illustrate this by completing a pay-off matrix.

| **Pay-off Matrix** | | | | |
|---|---|---|---|---|
| **Number of Wongos made** | **Market demand** | | | |
| | **400** | **600** | **800** | **1 000** |
| 400 | 8000 | 8000 | 8000 | 8000 |
| 600 | 6000 | 12 000 | 12 000 | 12 000 |
| 800 | 4000 | 10 000 | 16 000 | 16 000 |
| 1000 | −4000 | 8000 | 14 000 | 20 000 |

The figures in each square are obtained by working out what would happen for each choice of quantity manufactured and the (unknown) reaction of the market.

So, for example, if 400 Wongos are made, the result will be 400 × 20 = £8000 in *each* case – regardless of what the market will take.

The second row presents a different case. If 600 Wongos are made and demand is only for 400, then revenue will be reduced by stock-holding costs. Four hundred Wongos will be sold, while 200 will incur costs. The result will be 8000 – (200 × 10) = £6000. The remaining levels of sales will all result in 600 × 20 = £12 000.

Similar calculations will result in figures for the varying levels of production and sales as shown in the matrix.

## *Looking at the results*

The maximin (8000) and the maximax (20 000) outcomes are obvious in this case where a relatively simple situation is used to illustrate the concept. In real life there are likely to be production costs and other variables which will complicate the position – bringing the matrix into its own as an analytical tool.

Even in the simple case we have used, the effect of reaching or not reaching sales levels to meet output can be seen. People responsible for making output decisions can, if highly averse to risk, limit production to 400 Wongos and enjoy a revenue of

£8000. If they choose to take a braver decision and opt for 600 Wongos, they will have a chance of revenue of £12 000 – with a minimum of £6000 if the market demand is less than 600 but at least 400. Similarly, the optimists can see the size of the loss if 1000 Wongos are produced but only 400 sold.

The pay-off matrix is useful in many cases of high uncertainty as a means to show the limits of acceptable action and at least to avoid taking action which can result in heavy losses. The most optimistic decision-maker may draw back from making 1000 Wongos since a loss is on the cards and will settle for the safety offered by making 800. He will not be able to maximise and reach the £20 000 return, but he might make £16 000. At all events he will do no worse than £4000 – which is better than the shortfall of £4000 which he otherwise might experience.

# 3. MEAN, MODE AND MEDIAN

One of the simplest and most widely used forms of analysis is the calculation of the mean or average. By doing this one can produce one value which represents many values. The simple value is easier to comprehend and is convenient.

However, the average can be misleading. Take for example these values:

| |
|---:|
| 9 |
| 21 |
| 3 |
| 77 |
| 19 |
| 60 |
| **Total** = 189 **Average** = 31.5 |

In this case the average is not representative of any value in the group and gives no idea of what values appear in the group.

A little more indication is given if a range is added. The lowest figure in the group is 3 and the largest 77. If, therefore, the average is expressed as '31.5 within the range 3 and 77', the fact that 31.5 is not truly representative is recognised.

Averages are generally best avoided where the scatter of values is very wide and/or there are few values in the group. Notwithstanding this precaution, an average (or two averages) can yield useful guidance.

Suppose, for example, that information has been collected for, say, the number of bankruptcies occurring over a twelve-month period:

| | **Bankruptcies** |
|---|---|
| JAN. | 27 |
| FEB. | 26 |
| MAR. | 26 |
| APR. | 24 |
| MAY | 10 |
| JUN. | 17 |

| | |
|---|---|
| JUL. | 11 |
| AUG. | 19 |
| SEP. | 30 |
| OCT. | 31 |
| NOV. | 32 |
| DEC. | 40 |
| **Total** | 293 |
| **Monthly average** | 24 |

We could simply say that the average monthly figure is 24. This would give some idea of what is going on, but we can do better.

If we calculate the average of the first six months we get the answer 22.

If we now work out the average for the second six months we get 27.

This is 23 per cent greater than the average for the first six months – suggesting an upward trend.

The average for the last quarter (34) tends to confirm this calculation.

There may, of course, in a series of figures such as this, be seasonal or other factors to be taken into account, but the average, if cautiously used, can be useful. It is at least easy to calculate and *most* people know what it means.

## When is an average not an average?

The answer is when it means the most frequently occurring. For example, it was recently stated in a television interview that the average train was ten or more minutes late. What the speaker should have said was that *most* trains were ten or more minutes late.

The speaker could have been trying to say that trains were late by an amount of time which averaged to a figure in excess of ten minutes – or something like that!

Similar mistakes (and confusion) can result from using statements such as:

'The average salesperson . . .'
'The average machine . . .'
'The average customer . . .'

## The modal figure

The modal figure is the one which occurs most frequently and it can be a better guide in some cases when making a decision than the average.

It has been reported, for instance, that the modal size for men's shoes in Britain is 8. This is a particularly valuable piece of information for manufacturers and retailers of shoes. If the average had been calculated it might work out to, say, 8.7 which would be one of the most useless bits of information imaginable.

Of real practical value would be the modal figure for faults in domestic appliances. If the most frequently occurring fault is known it could have implications both for modifying the product and for the training of service engineers.

### *Grouping the modal figures*

It is often the case that there are several figures in a 'population' which are close to the modal one – sometimes even 'two modal figures'.

Suppose the errors made by a group of forty-two clerks were recorded. We might find something like this:

**Number of errors made**

| | | | | | | | | | | |
|---|---|---|---|---|---|---|---|---|---|---|
| 1 | 4 | 6 | 7 | 5 | 8 | 6 | 3 | 6 | 7 | 8 |
| 2 | 6 | 7 | 9 | 1 | 8 | 5 | 7 | 4 | 9 | 9 |
| 8 | 10 | 8 | 8 | 10 | 12 | 10 | 8 | 10 | 10 | |
| 9 | 5 | 10 | 9 | 10 | 9 | 11 | 9 | 9 | 10 | |

We could just take an average by totalling up all the errors made and dividing by 42. This results in an average of 6.5 errors per clerk. However, by no means all the clerks make as many mistakes as this and some made substantially more. The picture is made clearer by grouping the figures and looking for the mode:

| No. of mistakes | No. of clerks |
|---|---|
| 1 | 2 |
| 2 | 1 |
| 3 | 1 |
| 4 | 2 |
| 5 | 3 |
| 6 | 4 |
| 7 | 4 |
| 8 | 7 } |
| 9 | 8 } |
| 10 | 8 } |
| 11 | 1 |
| 12 | 1 |

The bracketed figures show that about half the clerks made 7 to 8 errors, with about another 10 per cent of them just above or just below this range.

This could have implications perhaps for a training programme, computerisation or changing the system. In particular, the modal figure can draw attention to the area where action is really needed rather than expending powder and shot over a wider target.

In the case of the clerks any corrective action could be concentrated on those scoring 8 or more mistakes. Even more guidance towards finding the solution to a problem might be gained by analysing the type of error made by the clerks. We might find a distribution like this:

| | |
|---|---|
| Incorrect code numbers | 6 per cent |
| Data omitted | 2 per cent |
| Discount wrong | 81 per cent |
| Total wrong | 11 per cent |

We might then say that the modal error is a miscalculation of the discount. If this is remedied in some way, the error problem is virtually eliminated.

In the event that there had been a larger number of types of error, the figures might be made more assimilable by constructing a bar chart which would draw attention visually to the guts of the problem.

## The median

The median is another kind of 'average' (from the Latin for 'middle') and, as its name suggests, is the value which splits a series of values in half. Suppose we have counted the number of calls made by salespeople over a given period. The results might be:

20 22 27 30 32 36 41

The median in this case is 30, i.e. there are an equal number of values on either side of it.

If there had been an even number of salespeople resulting in an even number of values recorded, the median would be halfway between the two middle values, e.g.:

20 22 27 30 32 36

The median would be:

$$\frac{27 + 30}{2} = 28.5$$

If the two middle values are the same then that value is taken as the median.

The mean, the modal figure and the median are all ways to try to represent – and put some sense into – the information you may have collected.

## Which one should you choose?

The mode is normally the most useful when we are examining categories – such as in the types of error example we looked at earlier.

Suppose we have done some research into industry preferences for the materials used as coatings for metal containers. We might have found the following:

| Preferred coating | No. of companies |
|---|---|
| Gloss paint | 20 |
| Matt paint | 16 |
| Bitumen | 8 |
| Wax | 6 |
| Varnish | 2 |
| No coating used | 1 |
| | 53 |

The modal coating is clearly gloss paint and it is the mode which is most significant as a representative figure. There would be no value, for instance, in working out an average by dividing the number of companies by the number of alternative coatings.

The average (that is the arithmetic average) comes into its own when there are 'quantity variables', particularly when a number of samples are taken from the same 'population'. In these cases the averages calculated are likely to be similar in size. The modes and medians will probably be more variable.

The median is useful when there is a value in a group which is out of line with all the others.

Suppose we have researched the expenditure of companies on training per employee per year. We have used a sample of ten similar companies in the same industry and recorded the following figures:

| £ |
|---|
| 1400 |
| 1500 |
| 1600 |
| 1950 |
| 2000 |
| 2150 |
| 2200 |
| 2250 |
| 2300 |
| 6700 |

The average for this group works out at 2405.

This average figure is distorted by the odd-ball tenth company who spend very much more than any of the others – nearly five times as much as the lowest spender.

The median figure (2075) gives a much more representative result and would give us a better idea of what the market has to offer if we were deciding whether or not to offer training services.

If there had been no odd-ball figure in the group, either the average or the median would have been reasonably representative. They would have worked out as:

Average – 1928
Median – 2000

In the event that you are dealing with a group of figures which includes an odd-ball you might consider excluding it, *providing* you can confidently explain the reason for the oddity, and be sure that it is the exception and unlikely to be duplicated.

In short, we apply some common sense and avoid ignoring a value simply because it may be convenient to do so.

## Moving averages

Mathematically simple, the moving average is useful in spotting trends.

A common application is in the analysis of sales figures where monthly sales, cumulative sales and a twelve-month moving average are used. There are, however, many other 'time-series' situations in which the moving average can be used, such as:

- accidents at the work place;
- machine failures;
- stockouts;
- customer complaints;
- on-target achievements.

### *How does it work?*

Suppose we have a series of values representing a number of monthly results – 4, 6, 10, 12, 14, 20. The first step is to group the number in pairs, namely:

4 + 6, 6 + 10, 10 + 12, 12 + 14, 14 + 20

and, by dividing the total of each pair by two, derive the averages as follows:

5, 8, 11, 13, 17

The new series of numbers generated is a moving average of the first series.

One of the effects of the calculation is to smooth out fluctuations – a result which becomes even more marked if the values are grouped in threes, fours or more.

### Why moving?

It will be noted that the oldest value (4) appears only once when paired. When the next month's value is known and added to the calculation, the oldest value is dropped and disappears altogether. The averages thus move in step with elapsed time.

# 4. DECISION TREES

Decision tree analysis is a useful technique in cases of uncertainty in so far as it puts some structure into the thinking of the decision-maker.

Using the decision tree technique is indicated in the following circumstances:

- where there are two or more choices of action which can be taken;
- where the choice made can result in further alternatives to be considered depending on the outcome of the first choice;
- where the expected results of taking the various and sequential decisions are significantly different in terms of likelihood and durability.

The name 'decision tree' is taken from the shape of a diagram which illustrates the situation and which is used as a framework to assess the probability and value of alternative outcomes. The basic diagram is shown in Figure 3.13.

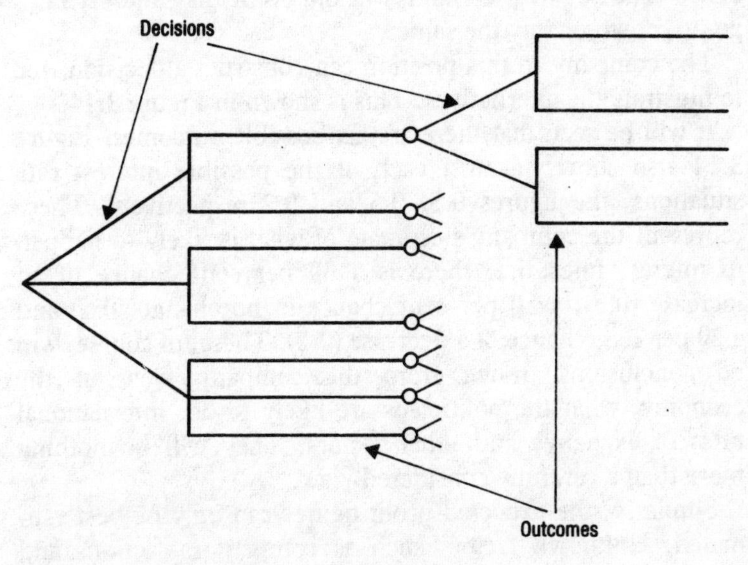


*Figure 3.13* The decision tree diagram

## What happens in practice?

The decision-maker considers the alternatives initially open to him or her and, using the information available, works out the likelihood of each of the possible outcomes and what these mean in, say, money terms.

The decision-maker must then follow through the implications of the possible outcomes in terms of the subsequent choices to be made and what their outcomes are likely to be.

The results of the calculating (or guessing) are then entered into the decision tree.

### *An example*

Imagine a company offering financial services. Two new services have been devised, but company resources are not sufficient to enable both to be launched. The problem of which to go for is further complicated in that both will be affected (to different extents) by movements in interest rates. Profits can be estimated with a reasonable degree of confidence (but not with certainty) in the event that interest rates go up, down or stay the same.

The company in this position can construct a decision tree to illustrate the alternatives. This is shown in Figure 3.14.

It will be seen that there are six possible outcomes. Figure 3.14 also shows, against each of the possible interest rate situations, the figures 0.3, 0.5 and 0.2 respectively. These represent the company's estimate of what is likely to happen to interest rates, i.e. there is a 30 per cent chance of an increase (0.3), a 50 per cent chance of no change (0.5) and a 20 per cent chance of a decrease (0.2). These, of course, will be conclusions drawn from the company view of the economy, what the politicians are likely to do, international rates of exchange and other factors. They will be nothing more than a carefully considered view.

Similarly, the expected profit figures can only be best estimated. Unknown factors such as competitors' actions and market response can only be guessed at.

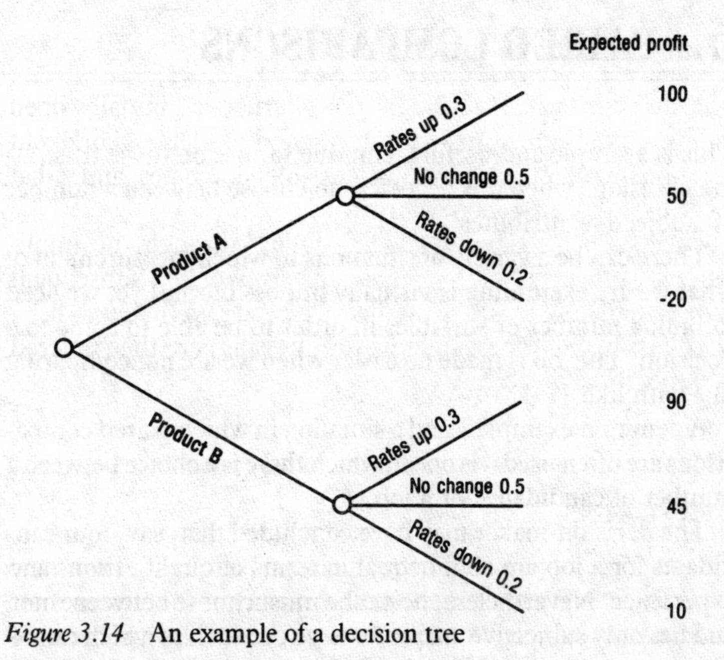


*Figure 3.14* An example of a decision tree

**What help is all this?**

Like most business decisions, this example is one which is surrounded by uncertainty. The decision tree will help by making sure that the problem is approached in a structured manner and forces the decision-makers to look at all the possible outcomes. It does not improve the quality of the guesses and estimates, but it does encourage logical thinking and more complete thinking.

In this example the company will at least have a strong indication that a loss will only occur if product A is chosen and interest rates go down. This might tip the balance of the decision in favour of product B which is expected to make a modest profit if interest rates fall.

Alternatively, since the company believes that there is an 80 per cent chance that rates will either stay the same or increase $(0.5 + 0.3 = 0.8)$, they might choose product A. If they do and rates increase they stand to make a higher profit than in the case of product B. The same applies if rates remain the same.

All in all, going through the discipline of this kind of analysis has a better chance of a successful outcome than mentally flipping a coin.

# 5. PAIRED COMPARISONS

This is a simple and useful technique for use on those frustrating occasions when it is necessary to choose between a number of 'subjective attributes'.

There can be a variety of situations in which measurement of what we are examining is virtually impossible and yet we need to rank a number of variables in order to be able to come to a decision. The job is made no easier when we are not comparing like with like.

A common example – and a situation in which paired comparisons are often used – is one in which there is a choice between a number of candidates for a job.

The decision-maker may have concluded that, say, four candidates for a job are about equal in terms of qualifications and experience. Nevertheless, he or she must choose between them and has only subjective attributes to go on, such as which candidate is most likely to 'fit in' with existing employees.

The task is made easier by comparing the candidates in pairs and putting the results in a simple matrix as shown:

| | MR W | MR X | MRS Y | MISS Z |
|---|---|---|---|---|
| MR W | | MR X | MRS Y | MR W |
| MR X | | | MRS Y | MISS Z |
| MRS Y | | | | MRS Y |
| MISS Z | | | | |

When comparing Mr W with Mr X the latter is preferred.

Mrs Y is also preferred to Mr W but Miss Z is not.

Mrs Y is preferred to Mr X and to Miss Z.

Miss Z is preferred only to Mr X.

The result is that Mrs Y is the favourite, having scored 3 squares on the matrix. This process can be related to one hard-to-measure attribute such as 'personality' and then repeated on, say, 'presence'. Alternatively, all the non-measurable attributes can be lumped together and a second round of comparisons made having eliminated the least preferred candidate.

This simple form of analysis can be used in such cases as:

- choosing between a number of designs for a logo;
- selecting advertisements from a range offered by an agency;
- deciding on decorating schemes for offices or showrooms;

or any other situation where it is necessary to put a relatively complex or intangible set of items in an order of preference according to any desired criteria.

# 6. ALGORITHMS

Algorithms can be used to work out what must be done in given situations. Their use has been defined as 'A rule for the solution of a problem in a finite number of steps'.

It is especially useful in highly complex situations where there is a multiplicity of possible actions *and the situations are strictly logical.*

The value in business situations is most marked where instructions are needed to ensure that the most appropriate action is taken when individuals are faced with choices of action. The algorithm can be written down as a series of questions or in chart form.

## A simple example

Imagine a company producing product for stock and product for immediate sale. When an order is received it could be for either type of product and could be required for immediate dispatch or not. The product could be available from stock or may need to be manufactured to meet the order.

Clearly, the company will want the order entry procedure to be such that each order receives the right treatment and that the right action is taken, whatever the circumstances.

Look now at Figure 3.15, which is an algorithm representing the decisions to be made depending on the nature of the order received. In real life the number of alternative courses of action available is likely to be greater and each of the actions more complicated. However, Figure 3.15 illustrates what an algorithm can look like.

The advantages in using it are:

- it helps to ensure that all the variables in a situation have been identified;
- it provides a 'checklist' of action to be taken step by step to arrive at an acceptable result.

It is not unusual where there is a mass of information to be

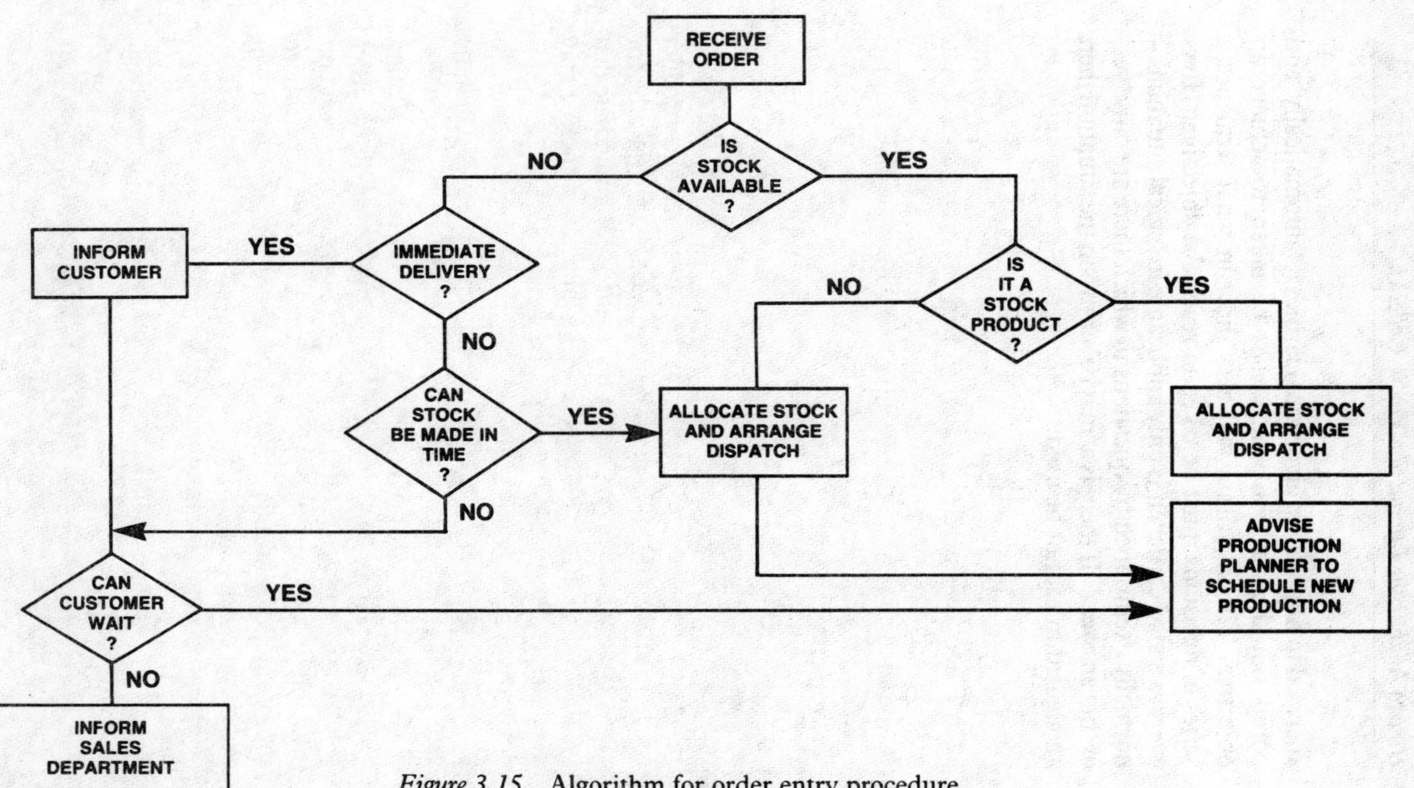


*Figure 3.15* Algorithm for order entry procedure

analysed to find that an algorithm clarifies it 'automatically' and points out the decision which *must* be taken to achieve an objective. The algorithm will also show in what sequence a series of decisions must be taken to reach the objective. However, as stated earlier, it is only applicable in logical situations – normally exemplified by questions to which there are only 'yes' or 'no' answers'. If there is a 'maybe' or two in the situation then an algorithm cannot be used.

# 7. OPERATIONS RESEARCH (OR) TECHNIQUES

Also known as operational research, OR techniques are based on a highly mathematical approach to analysis and consequent problem solving. Their use has tended in the past to be limited to a relatively few business people, because of the high degree of numeracy required. The situation is now changing rapidly because of the use of computer software which not only enables the calculations to be carried out more quickly, but also demands much less mathematical ability on the part of the decision-taker.

It is necessary though to have a basic understanding of the principles behind the techniques and the type of problems they are suitable for.

The following descriptions are designed to provide this basic understanding to give the non-mathematician a starting point for a selection of techniques.

OR techniques depend on building a mathematical model of the situation being analysed. The most widely applicable techniques are:

- linear programming;
- queuing theory;
- sequencing;
- sensitivity analysis;
- network analysis.

## Linear programming

This technique is not only widely applicable in solving business problems, but it is also one of the most powerful tools available to management. It can be applied wherever there is a problem of how resources should be used to obtain the best result – the classic application being the problem of how to decide on the best mix of ingredients in a product.

## *Example 1*

Suppose we are manufacturing, or intend to manufacture, a paint. The paint must contain a quantity of each of ingredient X and ingredient Y. There is, for each ingredient, a minimum and maximum figure, and there is a range of alternative mixtures which will result in a similar quality of paint. The costs of the ingredients differ. The problem is to work out the proportions which will result in the least cost (maximum profit) product.

Appropriate computer software will produce the answer – or, in many cases, the answers. There is likely to be a number of mixes which will optimise profits. A good computer program will illustrate the acceptable results in a graph such as the one shown in Figure 3.16.

Any combination of ingredients within the shaded area on the graph will produce a 'best' result.

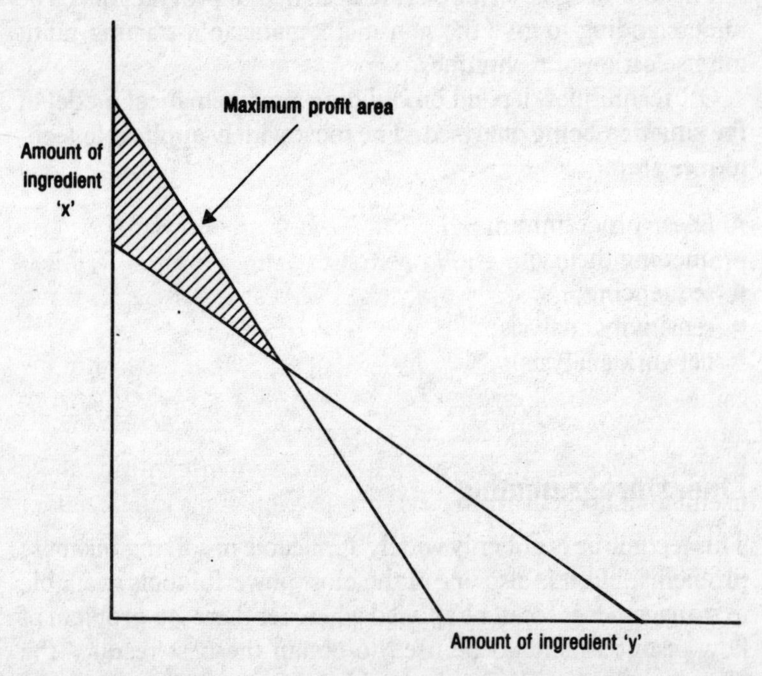


*Figure 3.16* Graphical representation of limitations on use of ingredients

### *Example 2*

A company manufactures a number of products. The profit on each is known. There are limits on production brought about by the need to share machine capacity and other resources such that, for example, the quantity of product A plus product B cannot exceed a certain amount.

The problem is to find the mix which meets the limitations of production resources and maximises profits.

A computer program, given all the necessary information, will first find any feasible solution. This will not necessarily be the most profitable solution and the computer will alter one of the variables to produce another feasible solution. The second solution will be compared with the first to see which is better. Then another variable will be tried and further comparisons made. Eventually by this process the best solution will be found.

The answer can, as in the first example, be illustrated graphically if required.

## In what other circumstances can linear programming be used?

According to British Standard 3527 linear programming is 'Any procedure for locating the maximum or minimum of a linear function which are subject to linear constraints and inequalities.'

This means, if you can translate BS 3527, that the technique can be used whenever the costs or the revenues resulting from any activity are proportional to the amount of that activity. Even if there is no exact proportionality, linear programming can be useful for all practical purposes if approximations can be made.

This opens up the field. The technique has been successfully used in such cases as:

- allocating the output of coal mines to a number of power stations;
- working out how sales representatives should best be allocated territories;

- calculating the amount of working capital required by a business, i.e. finding out how much money will be needed for operational purposes and capital investment in order to maximise profit while remaining solvent;
- determining which products should be bought in and which produced in-house;
- determining the optimum mix to maximise profits when a production unit is fully employed, but supply of raw materials for some products is limited.

## Queuing theory

There are many situations in which a queue will form. The obvious ones which spring to mind are customers waiting to be dealt with at supermarket checkouts, bank counters and post offices. Also familiar, although less obviously a 'queue', are customers waiting to be served in a restaurant.

An important consideration for businesses which experience such queuing situations is the extent to which provision for dealing with waiting customers is provided. Too many manned checkouts in a supermarket involves avoidable costs, but too few results in poor customer service.

Queuing theory provides a means to analyse what can be a complicated situation to provide an indication of the optimum service that should be provided. It is an attempt to reconcile the mutually exclusive requirements that there will be no delays in receiving attention, but at the same time those providing the service are never idle.

### *What information is needed?*

The following information about the situation to be analysed is needed.

#### The pattern of arrivals

This, in addition to people arriving at checkouts and the like, can involve goods arriving at loading bays or packaging equipment. It can include data arriving at a computer system for processing or parts moving down a production line for a further operation.

Life would be easier if, in all such cases, arrivals were regular and in a continuous, even flow. Unhappily, life is not like that and arrivals can be erratic – even random. In most cases, however, some pattern can be identified by observation and in some cases observation can result in the discovery of ways to even out the flow.

A useful way to illustrate the pattern of arrivals is to mark them on a simple time-scale such as this.

The arrival pattern illustrated above fits what happens at airports as passengers arrive to catch a flight. A few passengers arrive well ahead of the check-in time followed by an increasing number as the flight time approaches. The bulk of the passengers will arrive in the final fifteen to twenty minutes.

**The service rate**

This is the rate at which arrivals can be dealt with and is simply the average number of services which can be provided in a given period of time.

**The arrival/service ratio**

The arrival/service ratio (otherwise known as 'traffic intensity') is derived by dividing the average number of arrivals per unit of time by the average service rate per unit of time.

**The queue rules**

Most queues are dealt with on the basis of first-come, first-served. There may, however, be some priority given to some arrivals. For example, a computer system may give priority to sales invoices over all other transactions.

With this information available it is possible to work out (using established formulae) the answers to questions which can be vital to the business. Suppose, for example, that twenty cars arrive at a petrol station in a period of fifteen minutes. The arrival rate will be:

$$\frac{20}{15} = 1.3 \text{ per minute}$$

If the average service time is 1.5 per minute, then the probability that a customer will have to wait is $1.3 \div 1.5 = 0.86$.

In other words, there is an 86 per cent chance that a customer will have to wait. The average time that a car is in the queue (i.e. before service starts) is

$$\frac{0.86}{1.5 - 1.3} = 4.3 \text{ per minutes}$$

Given this information the business must decide whether or not the waiting time is acceptable, whether a longer wait could be tolerated or whether service levels need to be stepped up. The results of such analysis give the decision-maker something to go on rather than a vague feeling expressed in ways such as, 'Customers are having to wait too long' or 'We sometimes have too many customers waiting to be seated'.

Such observations or impressions need to be translated into quantitative terms before any reliable and cost-effective actions can be taken.

## Sequencing

Sequencing is a technique for working out the best sequence of activities to satisfy a given objective. For example, if a manufacturing company has a number of jobs to be done and each requires some time on various machines (or the attention of an employee), the number of alternative ways to schedule the work can be a substantial problem. Working out, say, the least costly sequence may be of prime importance.

If there are three jobs to be done and two machines to do them on there are thus thirty-six ways in which the work can be sequenced!

The number of alternatives is given by the formula:

$(n!)^m$ where n = the number of jobs and m = the number of machines

If, therefore, there are three jobs and three machines, the number of alternatives works out at:

$$(3 \times 2 \times 1)^3 = 6^3 = 216$$

When information on costs, deadlines, machine speeds etc. are added to the problem it is clear that finding the best solution is laborious to say the least when tackled with pen and paper. A computer package (which may require tailoring to suit your particular needs) can do the job in very little time.

The technique is not limited to manufacturing situations. It can also be used in office work where a mix of people and office machinery is involved. Possibilities include mail order operations, dividend warrant issues and share issues.

## Sensitivity analysis

Imagine a contractor about to submit a tender for building a bridge in a foreign country. Much work will have been done to work out the costs of labour, materials and the like. Equally, calculations will have been made as to how long the job should take.

If the job should overrun there may be a penalty clause and almost certainly an increase in costs. There are a substantial number of variables which can delay completion of the bridge and/or otherwise add to costs. They might include:

- labour shortages;
- strikes;
- bad weather;
- changes in interest rates;
- geological difficulties;
- shortages of materials.

There will be a substantial problem in deciding how to price the job and what completion date to quote given that no one knows which, if any, of the variables will adversely affect the job to be done. Clearly, the risk can be high.

Sensitivity analysis provides a means with which to come to some conclusion about the size of the risk (and the terms which can be offered) in a structured way.

## *Evaluating the variables*

All the variables should be listed and then, if there are many, they should be pruned down to the most significant half a dozen or so.

Each variable is then considered and a judgement made on the likelihood of something happening or changing. For example, we might conclude that it is feasible that bad weather could delay the project by 10 per cent, interest rates could rise by 15 per cent and unforecastable geological problems could add a further 5 per cent to costs.

These changes can now be fed into the computer and a number of 'What if' questions asked. For example:

- What if bad weather delays the project by 10 per cent?
- What if bad weather delays the project by 10 per cent *and* interest rates increase by 15 per cent?
- What if all the variables change adversely by 5 per cent?

and so on.

A different question can also be asked, namely 'What needs to happen to put the project at risk?'

Clearly, the accuracy of the whole exercise depends on (a) correctly identifying the key variables and (b) the accuracy of management judgement in deciding the possible limits of change to any variable.

However, the exercise goes a long way towards ensuring that the final quotation is based on calculated risk-taking and not pure gambling.

The results of the 'What if' questions will enable the decision-takers to make their decisions on the basis of an analysis of the best information available rather than a purely gut-feel reaction to a complex situation.

## Network analysis

Network analysis has become so common that it is now often excluded from a list of OR techniques. However, it is mathematical in nature and deals with complex situations, so it is not, in fact, out of place in such a list.

British Standard 4335 defines network analysis as 'A group of techniques for presenting information to assist the planning and controlling of projects. The information . . . includes the sequence and logical interrelationships of all project activities.'

There are two common types of network, namely:

- critical path method (CPM) and
- project evaluation and review technique (PERT).

### *Critical path method*

This type of network is used to identify the shortest route to the completion of a project by highlighting the activities which will delay the whole project if those activities are delayed. These activities are said to lie on the *critical path*.

#### An example of CPM

If a house is being built there will be certain activities which will dominate the completion date. The walls cannot be erected until the foundations have been completed and the roof cannot be put in place until the walls are finished. The foundations and the walls are thus critical and on the critical path. Other activities such as making the window frames would be pointless as a priority to the foundation and walls.

The critical path for a project is determined by constructing a diagram such as is shown in Figure 3.17.

The figures in brackets show the expected duration of each job and it is these periods of time which determine the critical path. Clearly, the completion date will depend initially on

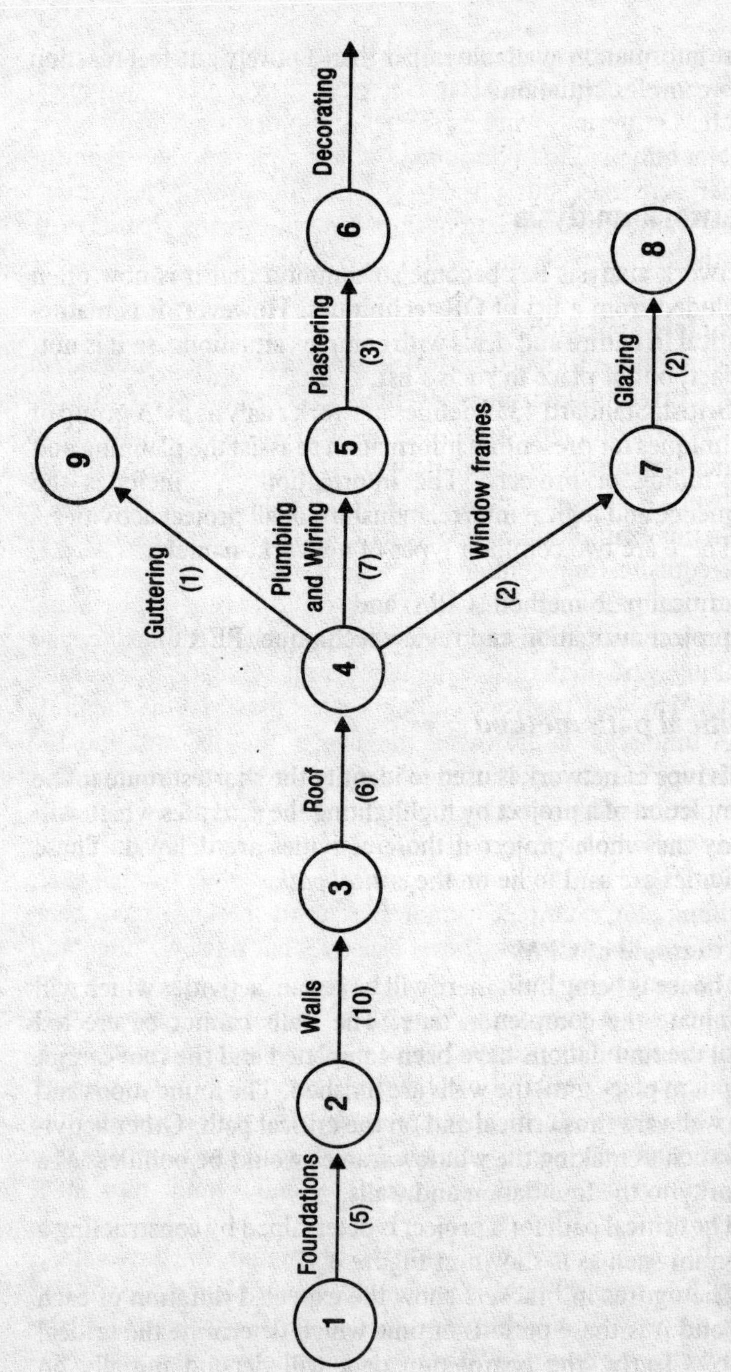


*Figure 3.17* Critical path network

concentrating resources on to the foundations, walls and roof. However, once the roof is finished there is a choice of activities, such as guttering, window frames and plumbing/wiring.

Not only will the plumbing and wiring take longer than the other activities, but plastering (and subsequent decorating) must wait for its completion. Plumbing and wiring are therefore on the critical path and should take priority.

**A simple approach**

A computer-produced network is probably unavoidable in major projects where possibly hundreds of actions are required. There are, though, a number of less complex situations in which a manually prepared network will suffice. The style of the network is also simpler and this is illustrated in Figure 3.18.

In this example we have two main actions to be completed as a prerequisite for opening a new supermarket. Staff must be ready and publicity effected. There could in practice be many other activities to be scheduled such as stocking the shelves and making sure that tills and other equipment are in working order. However, the two chosen aspects illustrate the method.

A time-scale is drawn on the side of the diagram and the activities are placed on the network according to the time that they are expected to take.

At the same time the dependency of one activity on another is made clear by the sequence. While it is obvious that staff training, for example, cannot start until the staff have been recruited, the network shows exactly what must be done and when it must be done.

The network is not only a means to plan things properly and to avoid spending precious time on work which can wait, but it also serves as a control mechanism. Once the project is under way, progress can be checked against the time-scale and the effect of any slippage is obvious. It is for reasons of slippage that a contingency time allowance is usually built into such networks.

CPM, in summary, will take the information you have gained (e.g. how long something will take to accomplish) and will sort out the way in which the project should be tackled, i.e. the answer to the question 'How do we go about this?'

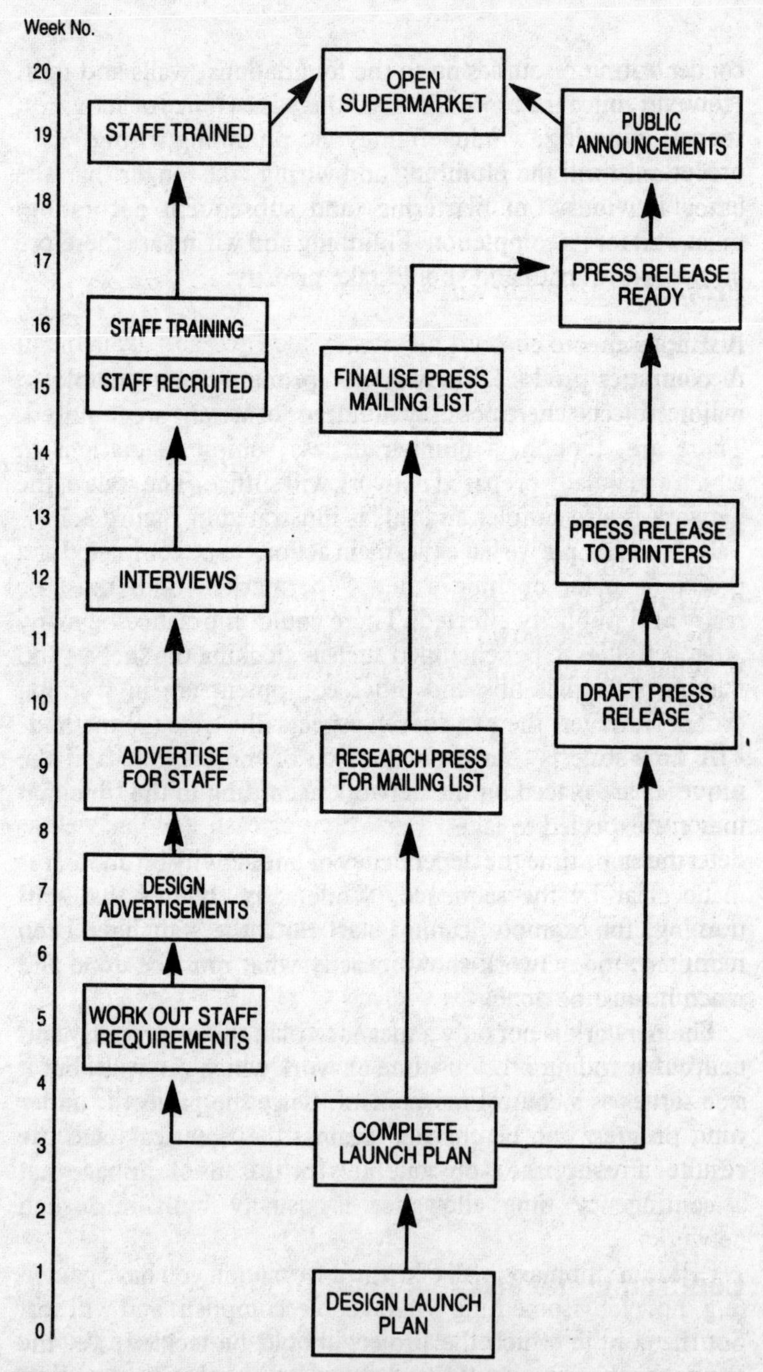


*Figure 3.18* A time-scale 'critical path' network

**By the way . . .**
It should not be imagined that networks are only applicable in the case of projects. They can be used also to analyse production processes and spot bottlenecks, thus perhaps solving the problem of low output rates.

## *Project evaluation and review technique (PERT)*

PERT takes into account the money required and available in the course of a project. At various stages of the work questions will need to be answered such as the following.

- We have budgeted for the cost of steel erectors. When will they be needed and when will they have to be paid?
- We budgeted to spend £10 000 next month on widgets. Is this figure still realistic?
- What will be the effect on payroll costs if pay rates increase by 7 per cent in two months' time?
- What is the effect on costs if there is a ten-day delay in finishing stage 3?

PERT, which has been described as a cost accounting technique, handles these and similar questions, and offers a means to control cash flow (or at least monitor cash flow) as well as determining the sequence of events.

The PERT network will identify those activities in which a delay will increase costs (e.g. for labour paid by the hour) and items which are not affected by delay (e.g. the purchase of a machine at the start of the project).

Before the project starts, running the network on the computer will provide a cash-flow picture and answer such questions as 'When will we need cash and how much?' Running the network again with changes based on performance results in revisions to the cash-flow picture.

## Confirming the problem definition

Sometimes the result of analysis will be an obvious solution to the problem. Sometimes the problem will be seen differently –

or a different problem will be seen. An apparent queuing problem may, after analysis, actually be seen as no problem at all.

A sensible and controlled backlog of work is an essential requirement for ensuring that resources are not lying idle and if it is found that the average waiting time is in fact so small as to be acceptable then analysis has disposed of the problem.

Confirming that there is indeed a problem or that the definition still holds good – or needs changing – is an essential step once analysis of the information is completed. There are of course some types of problem which cannot be solved until the cause is known. Fact finding and analysis of the facts to determine the cause is essential.

The next stage is to find a solution to the problem. This may be self-evident or relatively simple. It can also be difficult and time consuming and much may depend on the outcome.

Therefore, before entering the decision stage it is necessary to be absolutely clear exactly what you are deciding about.

Some final questioning should be carried out along these lines.

- Have we collected all the information which is relevant and available?
- Are there any assumptions or estimations we have made which could be verified or modified by more information?
- Have we thoroughly examined the information and analysed it in the right way – or sufficiently?
- Is there any way in which the originally defined problem can now be seen as an opportunity?
- Are we absolutely clear about what the problem is and have we identified the cause?

# PART 4

# Finding the Solution

Finding the solution to a problem often involves the taking of a decision. The process of making the decision is frequently mistaken for the process of problem solving which, as we have seen, requires the collection of information and its analysis as a prerequisite for effective decision-making.

If all the necessary information were to be available and properly analysed a decision would not be necessary since simple logic should give us the solution to the problem.

However, such a happy situation is rare in business life and the decision will probably involve risk, judgement and sometimes gut-feel.

## Let the solution develop

The first rule of successful decision-making is to allow the solution to develop. This means taking a look at the facts, figures and guesses available, and forming a view on what action to take. These first thoughts will probably be modified by discussion and challenge resulting in a development process until *an* answer is agreed on. In many cases there will not be an exactly right or wrong answer and the process should be allowed to result in one which is more or less effective and suited to the circumstances.

In other words do not be dismayed if perfection appears to be unattainable. Excellence is normally within reach.

## Make it rational

The intuitive thinking of an *experienced* person can be very effective in reaching the right decision. There is evidence though that getting it right on a hunch basis is getting harder as the business world becomes more complex and changes more quickly. It is also true that even if a hunch is the basis of a decision, the chance of success is greater if rational thinking is taken as far as the information available allows before resorting to the hunch.

Even if the information available is limited or of questionable accuracy it should not be ignored.

## Don't take the line of least resistance

The third requirement for reaching a conclusion is the avoidance of easy but self-defeating options. In particular, avoid the following common traps.

- Saying 'We will have a good look at this problem when we are not so busy.' That time will never come and the problem will stay with us.
- Saying 'We should find an expert to advise us.' This will take some time – after which any data we have collected will be out of date and the whole process will have to start all over again.
- Deciding that more information is needed before a decision can be taken – despite strenous efforts having already been made to collect the facts.

All these responses are often no more than ducking the problem in the hope that it will go away. While looking carefully before leaping may be good sense it must not be allowed to degenerate into putting off a decision indefinitely.

## The great new vista

A consultant carried out a six-month detailed study of some of the problems of a company. During the course of the study more problems and, more important, a number of opportunities were revealed.

The consultant presented his findings to a board meeting – the directors having already read his report.

During the course of a lengthy discussion a counter-proposal was put up for every proposal the consultant made. It gradually became clear to the consultant that the board lacked the will to grasp the nettles put in front of them. This was confirmed the next day when, after time to think the proposals over, the chairman expressed the views of his board. His comments were something like this:

> 'We find the report and proposals most interesting. The ideas put to us are thought provoking and new horizons have been opened to us. We will give them the closest possible consideration over the coming months and I will be appointing a sub-committee to examine each proposal in detail.'

The result? Absolutely nothing.

Action *was* taken much later as problems persisted and in some cases worsened. In the meantime damage was caused and some first-class opportunities were lost.

## The process of reaching a decision

Collecting the facts and analysing them is a form of diagnosis similar to that carried out by a doctor examining a patient.

Once the diagnosis is complete two more stages will follow:

- finding alternative solutions;
- evaluating and comparing the alternatives.

### *Finding alternatives*

The alternatives may involve two or more courses of action to resolve the problem, doing nothing or modifying the original objectives.

There are two techniques which are effective in finding workable alternatives when the facts do not make the required course of action obvious. These two techniques are brainstorming and the Delphi technique.

#### Brainstorming

This is not, as is sometimes believed, a think-tank session in which a group of people sit around with icepacks on their heads and coffee cups in their hands hoping for inspiration.

Brainstorming, when properly organised, is a structured process designed to stimulate creativity. It works in the following way.

**The brainstorming process**

A group of people – not necessarily comprising the decision-takers only – is selected. The group should represent a wide span of experience and knowledge of different aspects of the business. The following steps are taken.

**1.** All members of the group are fully briefed on the nature of the problem and whatever relevant information is available. They should all be clear about the objective to be achieved.

**2.** A 'leader' is appointed who will stand in front of the group armed with a fibre-tip marker (or similar) and a number of blank flip-chart sheets stuck around the walls.

**3.** The group now call out 'solutions' to the problem (i.e. alternative courses of action) and these are written on the flip-chart sheets by the leader.

*Note:* Two essential rules *must* be adhered to during the process of calling out solutions. First, *any* solution, however apparently silly, which comes into the head of a group member should be called out and recorded. This is a positive aid to creativity since a silly or impractical idea can stimulate a usable idea in the minds of others in the group.

In one brainstorming session someone shouted out 'Shoot the chief executive'. This, to some an attractive idea, was not a feasible proposition, but it led to some highly relevant suggestions regarding the role of the chief executive and his senior colleagues.

Second, there must be no comment whatsoever on any of the ideas called out. It is human nature to find fault in other people's ideas and in any brainstorming group there will be people tempted to respond with comments like 'That's a silly idea', 'That will not work' or 'Too costly'.

Adverse comment can kill creativity stone dead and the flow of ideas will dry up in seconds – especially if the chief executive is the person who makes the adverse comment.

Interestingly, a brainstorming session is the one place

where counter-proposals are useful – as is any idea which enters someone's head.

4. After a time (usually ten to twenty minutes) the flow of ideas will dry up and the calling-out session can be brought to an end. The group can now turn its attention to the collection of ideas written on the flip-chart sheets. The obvious nonsense ideas can be crossed out, as can anything which is, *without doubt*, either irrelevant or unattainable. This should leave a short-list of alternative courses of action which are worthy of serious consideration. In a session of fifteen minutes or so anything up to forty ideas are likely. Of these it would be disappointing if there were not four or five worthy of serious evaluation.

## *Evaluating and comparing the alternatives*

This need not be a complicated procedure but it should be a disciplined and structured one. There is a tendency among human beings when faced with, say, three or four alternatives to choose one on a subjective basis. We are all attracted by the option which will involve us in the least effort, hassle or change. This may, of course, be the worst option for the business and we let the best alternative go.

The essential requirement for avoiding the subjective choice is to prepare a pros and cons list.

### The pros and cons

Suppose a company is planning to expand its sales activities into a foreign country. The company could:

- set up a subsidiary in the foreign country;
- appoint a local sales agent; or
- use its own representatives who will travel to and from the new market.

A pros and cons list for deciding which is the best option will look something like this:

| Factors | Subsidiary | Agency | Representative |
|---|---|---|---|
| 1. Set-up cost | £50 000 | nil | nil |
| 2. Running cost | £100 000 p.a. | 10% of sales | £40 000 p.a. |
| 3. Estimated sales | £200–300 000 | £100–200 000 | less than £100 000 |
| 4. Control | High | Low. Agent may give notice | High |
| 5. Other | Local staff to be found and trained | Agent uses own staff. Has local knowledge | No continuous presence. No local knowledge |

Items 1 and 2 in the list are tangible facts which, with adequate research, can be depended on.

Item 3 is a semi-tangible and in each case is a best estimate based on some market research.

Items 4 and 5 are intangible and cannot be expressed in quantitative terms. Despite this, each of these factors has a value which must be assessed in some way and taken into account. For example, if the business is set up using an agent and the agent for some reason pulls out (or goes bust) the business could grind to a halt. Similarly, while a wholly owned subsidiary will result in a high degree of control of what goes on, it will cost money to set up, and finding local staff – and training them – could be a headache.

A mixture of such tangible and intangible considerations is a common and frustrating situation. However, this is where the Delphi technique comes in as a means to reach a conclusion.

**The Delphi technique**

The hunch, gut-feel, judgement – call it what you will – of the decision-makers will be required whenever there is an intangible element in the equation. It is necessary to ensure that the judgement is a sober one and not influenced either by undue optimism or undue pessimism. It should not be subject to, for example, a single past experience (good or bad) of one person who might allow the experience to sway him or her unreasonably in one or other direction.

Likewise, an individual may be influenced by some personal objective into ignoring or playing down an element in the mixture. Someone with an ambition to run a subsidiary might support setting one up even if it is not the best solution from the company point of view.

The Delphi technique is a means to make maximum use of the judgemental skills of a group of people and also to smooth out any personal bias which might lead to a poor choice.

This is how to use the technique.

**1.** A group of experienced people with a wide range of skills is brought together.

**2.** The decision to be taken is explained to them and each person is given all the available facts, estimates and any other aspects to be taken into consideration.

**3.** Time is allowed for each participant to study the information provided and the opportunity is given to them to ask questions to clarify anything they are unsure about. *But, note, no debate or discussion should take place between the participants.*

**4.** When everyone is ready they are asked to write down their preferred alternative on a piece of paper – without allowing any other participant to be aware of their choice.

**5.** The votes are now added up by an 'umpire'. Let us suppose that the votes in the case of the overseas market problem were:

| | |
|---|---|
| Agency | 6 |
| Subsidiary | 4 |
| Representative | 2 |

The umpire will announce that the representative route is the least favoured option and that this choice will now be discarded. The umpire will *not* reveal the number of votes awarded or the fact that agency was the favourite.

**6.** A second round of voting now takes place to choose between the remaining alternatives.

**7.** The second round of votes is counted up and if there is a clear preference this is announced and becomes the company choice. If there is no clear preference (avoidable by having an odd number of participants), an open debate can be held, followed by a further vote.

Sometimes, though not often, the preferences are so evenly balanced that it is necessary to collect more information. This is not always possible due to time pressures or lack of resources, so a casting vote can be made by the most senior or most accountable person.

**Why not tell people the results of the first vote?**
Another strong human tendency is to join a bandwagon. If we know that six people voted for setting up an agency and we were among the minority who preferred a subsidiary we might be influenced by a desire to join the majority. We might feel that the majority must be right and will stop looking at the information objectively.

**What does Delphi do for us?**
First of all it brings together the combined intuitive skills of several people. These intuitive skills should not be regarded as being of no value simply because they are intuitive. Our gut reactions to situations are the result of many past experiences – some long forgotten – which we nevertheless store away in our brains. Our reactions, even if we are not conscious of it, are governed by a lifetime of learning – the result of which is intuitive (almost instinctive) behaviour governed by the information stored away.

Delphi allows this past experience and learning to be brought to bear on the problem, but in a way which is:

- modified by the experiences of others; and
- influenced by at least some quantitative data (even if only estimations) as a result of collecting information and analysing it at an earlier stage.

Delphi also avoids one of the main dangers when a group is considering what to do – going along with the most influential member of the group. It is hard to avoid agreeing with the boss or perhaps some lesser person with a powerful voice and personality. The secrecy of the vote and the absence of any debate before voting eliminates this factor and encourages individual thinking.

**Don't overlook the other consequences**

Stress was laid on giving the Delphi group a thorough briefing before they cast their votes. This briefing should include an assessment of the side-effects or consequential effects of the courses of action being considered.

Quite often in problem solving a single-minded determination to reach a particular objective can result in other important aspects being overlooked.

An example of this occurred in Bermuda when the authorities were trying to find a solution to the problem of too many cars on the island.

Bermuda, with its narrow roads and generally limited space, was feeling the effects of an affluent society where everyone wanted a car. There were already regulations limiting the size of car which could be used in Bermuda, but it was clear that some further action was needed.

A regulation was brought in limiting each household to one car. This caused a housing shortage!

Accommodation had always been hard to come by on the island and it was customary for young couples to live with their parents for the first few years of marriage. This, under the new regulation, meant that they could not have a car if the parents already had one. The result was a marked increase in the demand for houses as young people now wanted to set up home separately in order to be able to have a car.

## Can it be done sequentially?

Sometimes the full impact and consequences of a decision are extremely difficult to foresee. Sometimes, also, the action to be taken can be broken down into two or more parts. If so it may be desirable to implement the first part and see what happens before implementing the next part.

This approach is often seen in the selection of people for promotion. The Peter Principle tells us that everyone is promoted to his or her level of incompetence, but one way of at least delaying this unhappy result is to 'promote in stages'.

Suppose that there is a need to replace a senior person who will retire in two or three years' time. The choice of a replacement could be a tough one and it may not be a good idea to recruit from outside the company. In such situations it is often the case that a particular person is seen as a likely candidate, but there may be doubts.

The first step might be to appoint the favoured person as deputy to the retiring executive and see how he or she matches up. If all goes well a part of the responsibilities of the job can be handed over completely and a further assessment made after a suitable period of time.

While failure will be an uncomfortable result, it is easier to handle at one of the stages than if the new person were just given the vacant job and then found to be unsuitable. This principle can be used in any situation where consequential effects are hard to forecast or evaluate. 'Try it and see' can limit any damage resulting from the wrong choice of action.

## Utterly baffled – a case for creative thinking

Brainstorming is a process which aids and stimulates creative thinking – defined as 'the use of the subconscious mind in problem solving situations'. It is what is needed when, despite careful fact-finding and analysis, no one has a clue what to do.

Edward de Bono recommended lateral thinking as a means to resolve such situations – that is to examine the problem from an unusual angle. He said, 'If traditional or vertical thinking is digging the same hole deeper, lateral thinking is digging a hole in a different place.'

### *Flying in the face of logic*

The medical authorities in a West African country were, some years ago, faced with a problem of a marked increase in deaths caused by sleeping sickness. This disease is spread to humans by various species of the tsetse fly which lives in damp and shady places – primarily in the vegetation lining the banks of streams.

It had been found that farmers were growing rice in the wet areas adjacent to the streams and this was bringing them into more frequent and prolonged contact with the tsetse flies. Various solutions to the problem were suggested, including banning the growing of rice. This was considered neither democratic nor feasible, and an alternative of a mass injection scheme was too expensive and of doubtful effectiveness. The possibility of killing the tsetse flies by spraying with insecticide was also ruled out on the grounds of costs and its effect on the evironment in general.

It seemed to the authorities that they were facing an insoluble problem.

**The lateral solution**

After months of agonising and debate someone came up with some lateral thinking which solved the insoluble problem. The farmers would be encouraged to grow *more* rice!

The fact was that in order to grow the rice the farmers first cleared away the vegetation in which the tsetse flies lived, so if the farming was on a wider scale all the vegetation would go rather than the small patches which left tsetse-infested areas on either side of them.

Free rice seed was issued to the farmers and the next planting season saw the mass destruction of the tsetse habitat. Within a year the problem was solved – at very low cost and with no social problems.

## What encourages creative thinking?

It is a common fallacy that brilliant new ideas descend on 'creative people' like manna from heaven just when they need it. With cries of 'Eureka' the discoverer of a great new truth leaps from his bath to tell the world.

The fact is that the flash of inspiration normally results from a long period of working on the problem and collecting the information surrounding it. It has been said that Charles

Goodyear discovered how to vulcanize rubber 'when he accidentally spilled some crude rubber on a stove'. This popular conclusion ignores the fact that Goodyear had been working on the problem for some years, had carried out many experiments and could readily recognise what happened when he spilled his crude rubber. The discovery was not a one-off event, but rather was one connected with much exploration and thinking during earlier years.

Psychologists and other experts seem, over the years, to have agreed that there is a creative process made up of four parts. These are as follows.

- **Saturation** This means becoming fully familiar with the nature of the problem and all the surrounding information.
- **Deliberation** This is a phase of digesting information and considering various ideas. Possible solutions are analysed, challenged and perhaps rearranged.
- **Incubation** In this stage the problem solver is reckoned to 'switch off', relax and allow the subconscious mind to work.
- **Illumination** This is the flash of inspiration stage where a bright idea is hit upon. The idea (growing *more* rice) may seem a little crazy at first sight, but there is a sense that it may be the answer.

This four-stage process is probably an accurate description of what does actually happen. The problem for business people is that there is rarely enough time – especially to deliberate and incubate. We may have the facts (or at least some of them) and the decision is needed this week, this day or even within the hour.

There is, for example, little time to sit back and ponder, let alone to switch off, if our company is faced by a sudden and hostile takeover bid. In such cases action is needed 'yesterday' and there will be little room for error.

## *Speeding up the process*

Brainstorming is one technique for accelerating the stages, but it may not always meet our needs.

We may need something more, including ways to overcome three barriers to creative thinking, namely, habit, complacency and apathy.

**Habit**

The philosopher and psychologist William James said, about habit, in 1890, 'It dooms us all to fight out the battle of life upon the lives of our early choice, and to make the best of a pursuit that disagrees, because there is no other for which we are fitted and it is too late to begin again.'

Habit is expressed as 'The way we do it here', 'We always do it this way' or 'It is company policy'.

All these are expressions of the habit obstacle to finding a solution to the problem. Habit is sometimes seen in the form of a sacred cow such as the one beloved by a managing director who insisted that his company should never use window envelopes as 'they are bad for the company image'. Persistence with this sacred cow meant that mass mailings were a costly headache as every envelope had to be individually addressed. The associated problems of cost and delay were not solved until he retired and automatic folding and envelope stuffing machinery could be used.

Habit can be overcome when it is (1) recognised as such and (2) challenged. The system analysis questions (what, where, when, how and why) come into their own in both regards.

Try this checklist – or something similar tailored to your own business or problem – to break down habit obstacles to your decision-making progress.

- Why do we do this? What is the reason?
- Is the reason really valid?
- Can we modify our policy, ideas, product (or whatever) and gain by doing so?
- Can we combine two things, e.g. two purposes or two processes?
- Can we rearrange things, e.g. is there another sequence or schedule we can use? Can we speed something up or slow it down?

- Is there a substitute, e.g. another product, raw material, place, person, process?
- What happens if we reverse things? Must we make X before Y or wait for someone else to move first?

**Complacency and apathy**

These are often the result of many years of profitable trading with no real threat to the business. The easy years encourage the belief that it is OK to carry on as before and that problems, if ignored, will go away. The way round this is to indulge in a little brain-washing.

First, remind yourself of what happened to Rolls-Royce in the early 1970s, Laker Airways, ILG, Coloroll, Polly Peck and other high flyers – all now crashed.

Second, ask yourself the question, 'If I owned the company would I sit on my backside and just let things drift on?'

If there is still some complacency or apathy to overcome make a list of all the awful things that could happen to the company and cost them out.

In one company a perceived threat to a part of the business was being ignored by some of the older executives. A less complacent executive worked out that if the threat became a reality and if a similar thing happened in the same year to *any other* part of the business it would spell disaster. A vision of the end concentrates the mind, especially when it is made clear that the end may actually be nigh.

## Speeding up the incubation period

One of the obstacles to obtaining the flash of inspiration is becoming mentally bogged down with the problem. After a time the mind becomes set in a rut of one-track thinking and the solution ever more elusive. A way to break out is to do something which, on the face of it, may seem to be a waste of time.

## *A walk in the park*

The author was once a member of an organisation and methods team working in London near to St James's park. The members of the department were constantly involved in finding the solutions to problems – some of which were very elusive.

A practice developed in the department of going for a walk when creativity seemed to have dried up. It was said (and it worked) that one circuit round St James's park was enough to bring out the answer to a simple problem, two circuits for difficult problems and three circuits for the real stinkers.

Some people were shocked at this behaviour which was contrary to the convention that if you are not sitting at your desk then you are not working. This of course is nonsense. If going for a walk gets results then do it.

There is also some evidence that physical activity of any kind may stimulate the mental processes, so if you are in a rut why not go swimming or take a session in a gym or perhaps just stroll round the block?

## Don't reinvent the wheel

There are very few problems which have not, in some form or another, cropped up somewhere before. It is also likely that someone else has *solved* them before.

Your company and its difficulties will not be unique, however much you may like to think so. Ask yourself these questions.

- What other companies will have had a problem like this? How have they solved it? Can you not ask them?
- Is the problem and its solution likely to be known by a business school or other academic organisation who could help with advice?
- Can your trade association, the CBI, British Institute of Management or the local chamber of commerce provide the answer?

It may be the case that a similar, even if not identical, problem has been solved by someone else and looking at the way they tackled it could put you on the right track.

There is unhappily another emotional block which can be encountered when looking at how other people did it and one which is not confined to any particular national group. This is as follows:

### *'They have all got two heads'*

The development manager of an international company was examining problems which involved a number of departments located in different countries in Europe. Each department did much the same job for the company within their own national boundaries.

It was found that a particular problem had been well and truly solved in the German part of the company and the development manager explained to the French, Dutch and Belgian departments how the Germans had done it. This ready-made solution was expected to be welcomed with open arms. Sadly, this was not the case.

The French refused to discuss the subject. The Belgians argued that conditions in Germany were *wholly* different (this was demonstrably untrue) and the Dutch manager dismissed the idea with the remark that 'All the Germans have two heads'.

This sad episode was a classic case of the 'not invented here' syndrome. This is a form of self-destructive pride which prevents people from taking advantage of someone else's good idea.

## The bite-at-a-time approach

It is impossible for anyone to sit down and eat a whole roast ox in one go. This does not mean that the ox can never be eaten by one person. If it is made into 200 hamburgers and two are consumed each day, then the problem of eating the ox is dealt with in 100 days.

This principle of separating a problem into components is known by the jargon term 'resolution' and it can stimulate creativity. The immensity of a problem can be such that the mind boggles at finding a solution. However, if it is broken down into several smaller parts, the problem becomes not only more manageable, but ideas for its solution are more likely to emerge.

A variation on the theme is 'Synectics', taken from a Greek word meaning 'the fitting together of diverse elements'. In some ways similar to brainstorming, a 'synectic group' will examine and talk about a key aspect of a problem. Novel ideas are sought by encouraging the group to fantasise and then to concentrate on one idea at a time relating to the aspect of the problem being addressed.

Participants in a synectic group must have prior training in the technique and the group must be led by an expert. This makes the technique more difficult to employ, but it can deal with more complex problems than brainstorming and has been effectively used in highly technical situations.

## Using the devil's advocate technique

Creativity can be stimulated by pressure and confrontation. Since everyone knows someone in their organisation who is only too willing to argue the toss over any imaginable subject, finding the pressure and the confrontation normally turns out to be easy.

The devil's advocate technique is particularly useful when the problem is intractable, but you are halfway to a solution. You know that the solution is imperfect, but getting it into shape has defeated you.

This is how to go about it.

- Get your 'solution' together as if it were the right one for the job.
- Find a suitably cynical, argumentative (even difficult) person and put the 'solution' to him or her as if you are feeling satisfied with it.
- Encourage, if necessary, the devil's advocate to comment on your 'solution'.

- When the criticisms come you must defend them to the hilt. Justify everything you have put forward and don't give in.
- For every adverse comment made by your opponent ask the question 'OK, but what would you do?' Most devil's advocates will be happy to tell you – and you can then force them to justify their idea.

This process can go on for as long as the two adversaries can stand it – or until you have found what you are looking for. The result is normally a list of new ideas. Some will have come from the devil's advocate and some from you. The effect of the confrontation is to trigger new lines of thought in both people. Each line of thought can lead to yet more ideas and so on.

Of course, the same technique can be used when you firmly believe that you really do have the solution to the problem. The devil's advocate may well find, or prompt you to find, a weakness in your idea. This can save a lot of wailing and gnashing of teeth at a later stage.

## Look back at the discards

It is often the case that a number of potential solutions to a problem will quickly be discarded in the early stages of seeking the answer.

It is not unknown for one of these abandoned ideas (possibly modified) to turn out to be the solution needed. The first ideas put forward are more prone to be rejected on emotional grounds and also because the team considering them will be hoping for a more perfect solution. When an idea is clearly less than perfect, or would present difficulties in implementation, it is likely to be set aside. It must not, however, be forgotten. The chances are that when it is found that there is no perfect solution the team will be willing to re-examine the early ideas, find ways to overcome any associated obstacles and mould one of them into shape.

## Encouraging creativity – a summary

- Use brainstorming to stimulate ideas – but do it properly in an organised way and don't allow any comments on the ideas generated.
- Use the Delphi technique to make best use of the experience of the people involved and to avoid the gut-feel of one person overriding the gut-feel of all the others.
- Try lateral thinking when you are in a hole.
- Challenge anything that is blocking a line of action because it is 'company policy' or because 'we always do it that way'.
- Don't let complacency or apathy dull your senses. Work out what could happen if your problems persist or worsen. It may be *you* who ends up out of a job.
- Do unconventional things. If ideas come to you when hill-walking then do it. If your boss objects to this use of your time ask for his or her solution to the problem!
- Don't exhaust yourself trying to solve a problem which has been solved already somewhere else. Ask other organisations what they have done and don't let pride stand in your way. It is not smart to waste time reinventing the wheel.
- Try the bite-at-a-time approach when faced with a very large problem. Breaking the problem down makes it easier to cope with and less of a psychological barrier to creative thinking.
- Make use of your argumentative colleagues. Get them to act (knowingly or otherwise) as devil's advocates. The confrontation will stimulate new thoughts.
- Look back at ideas that you have abandoned. Do they deserve a rethink? Can one of them be modified and made to suit your purpose? Can two of them be combined?

## What kind of management style encourages creativity?

The manager of the financial department of a major British company complained that his staff were dull and apathetic. The reasons were obvious to a trained observer.

- The manager was a martinet who would 'not tolerate mistakes'. The result was that everyone took the safe route, changed nothing and did exactly as they were told.
- All decisions were taken by the manager who did not consult his staff.
- Any ideas put forward by staff were promptly shot down – usually with a comment such as 'you are not paid to think'. The result was that the staff stopped thinking.

This manager epitomised almost everything that inhibits creativity and progress.

A style which encourages ideas and innovations (and thus makes work more interesting for everyone) will have the following characteristics.

1. All staff feel responsible for the progress and prosperity of the department or company – and not just the boss. This is achieved by building a *team* as opposed to a collection of workers and in particular by:
   - informing staff of what is going on, problems, achievements, plans and objectives;
   - encouraging discussion and debate at all levels and between levels;
   - listening to and carefully examining any suggestions put forward by staff.

2. Staff at all levels are involved and participate in problem analysis and decision-making.

3. Decisions are encouraged at all levels and are not the sole preserve of the boss. Decision-taking is delegated to the lowest possible level in the 'hierarchy' as is practicable.

4. Staff are encouraged to take action on their own initiative and, when mistakes occur, are supported in correcting them and not punished for making them.

5. The manager's door is always open – or even better removed from its hinges and dumped in the nearest skip!

Check how your own management style matches up to these criteria.

# Part 5

# Ways to Make the Solution Work

It is not unknown for a solution to a problem to emerge from careful fact-finding, thorough analysis and a good deal of careful consideration only to result in nothing really happening.

There is a tendency among busy executives, having agreed on what to do, to heave a great sigh of relief and move on to another pressing topic or back to routine work – without ensuring that what they have decided will, in fact, be implemented.

It is not enough just to agree on the action to be taken and then assume that it will be taken. There are many reasons why the whole thing may disappear into oblivion including:

- no one is clearly responsible for taking the action agreed on;
- authority is not placed where it is needed;
- no plan is prepared for implementation, e.g. with clear deadline dates for completion of the various stages;
- no funds are allocated and the whole thing gets bogged down in a welter of accounting bureaucracy;
- the action required is not properly communicated and there are varying (and probably conflicting) notions as to what should happen;
- there are opponents to the plan who successfully block action – often covertly and by means of a form of 'passive resistance'.

Virtually any one of these deficiencies can result in failure – if not in the sense that nothing happens but, alternatively, in the sense that what does happen is not that which was intended.

## The familiar computer system problem

Disappointment with the results (or lack of them) is a common experience with the implementation (and attempted implementation) of a computer system. Many businesses have been through a frustrating cycle of events only too familiar in recent years.

- Management are persuaded or persuade themselves that their problems will all be over if a computer system is installed.

- With great hopes (even euphoria) plans are drawn up and orders placed for hardware and software.
- Departments and individuals are given dates by which they can expect their part of the system to be installed.
- Time goes by and so do the dates for installation – with no sign of the computer system.
- Revised dates are announced and in the meantime staff become unsettled and the old system (now not receiving any investment) gets worse.
- Requests are made for more resources. Programming is running behind and more programmers are demanded.
- More expenditure is resisted or refused and the system is down-graded. Compromises are found, and bits and pieces are lopped off the system to cheapen it and hasten implementation.
- Eventually a system (not *the* system) is installed. Users are disappointed because they are not getting what they expected, confidence wanes and the system falls into disrepute.
- After a few weeks it is agreed that the system is not producing the results originally expected and more powerful hardware is demanded.
- Management agonise over the additional and non-budgeted cost and wonder why it all went wrong . . .

## *The process for getting it right*

Whether the action to be taken is brief and simple, or lengthy and complex, the same steps must be taken if there is to be any reasonable certainty of success. The only essential difference between implementing a major change and implementing a minor one is in the volume of detail to be taken into account. It is the degree of attention to the detail which, in most situations, determines whether or not the objective is achieved.

The starting point for success is, in implementation, exactly the same as it was in finding the solution to the problem in the first place – defining your objective. This requires some thought as to *how the objective will be expressed*. Many great schemes have come to grief simply because insufficient attention was paid to the detail of the objective.

## How not to express your objective

Avoid at all costs objectives which do not pin down exactly what you want. A bad objective would be 'To speed up the dispatch of invoices', or 'To reduce bad debts' or 'To cut wastage'.

Worthy though these ambitions may be, they tell you nothing more than the fact that you want an improvement (apparently any old improvement) in an unsatisfactory situation.

Consider the objective of speeding up the dispatch of invoices. If it currently takes ten days to get the invoices out of the door, we will have achieved our *stated* objective if we cut the time to nine and a half days. Is that what you wanted? The chances are that you were really thinking about five days (or even less), but if you don't say so and then base all your actions on this value, then you are very likely to fail.

The bad debts position will be improved if outstandings over ninety days are brought down from £100 000 to £99 995. Your credit controller can now relax. He or she has achieved the stated objective.

Likewise, if wastage is cut from 5 per cent to 4.99 per cent, another objective has been achieved – without actually making any real impact on the problem to be solved.

## Cosmetic changes

A British company wasted the time of two senior executives for about two years by failing to spell out an objective in quantitative terms. It had been agreed that there was a productivity problem and it was clear that changes in working methods and possibly in organisation were required. The two executives were given the job of finding and implementing the changes, but without any clear objective. One of the executives actually asked for a clear statement of objectives, but was told that this was not necessary on the grounds that 'we all know what we need'. It was also argued that spelling out the objective would 'restrict the freedom of action' of the two people.

The reverse was in fact the case. Since there was no positive aim in view, the various heads of departments could not be persuaded to co-operate to any significant degree. The result was a series of *cosmetic* changes which, after two years' work, added up to nothing worth while. The problems were still there two years later when another team was launched to try to solve them.

Sadly, despite the previous experience, no clear objective was laid down for the second attempt and at the time of writing the team is still wallowing around trying to decide what to do.

## *Spell it out in detail*

Let us consider the use of a computer service chosen as the solution to a problem. How should the objective be expressed?

Let us assume that the original problem to be solved was one of levels of output. In a real-life case a company providing a service was offered a contract with a large organisation to handle certain transactions for them. The volume of work was expected to double as the result of the new contract and it was obvious that existing resources would be insufficient to cope. Increasing the number of employees was rejected as a solution and a computer system was decided on.

The objective was stated as follows:

**1.** A computer system is to be installed and be fully operative by 2nd January 1991.

**2.** The system will include the following.
- A database of client details. The database will enable access to be gained within thirty seconds by any employee.
- Automatic production of sixteen standard letters, debit notes, credit notes and acknowledgements.
- Accounting records showing all cash movements with running totals and monthly summaries.

**3.** The system will come into operation in these stages:
database by 1 November 1990
standard documents by 1 December 1990
Accounting records by 2 January 1991.

This objective (which in real life was backed up by a note detailing accounting headings and the like) has the merits of stating not only what should happen but by when. A standard of performance was also laid down for access time to the database.

Details such as these enable those responsible for the designing and installation of the system to know what in *real* terms is required of them which in turn enables them to design a plan to meet the requirements. Management, by setting standards and deadlines, has a yardstick against which progress can be measured.

## The characteristics of a good objective – a summary

A good objective will satisfy five criteria.

**1.** It will be relevant and 'well researched'. This means that all aspects of the objective will have a direct bearing on the problem to be solved and will not be weakened by add-ons which divert efforts away from the primary purpose.

It will be carefully thought through with adequate consultation with involved and affected people whose opinions will be taken into account.

**2.** The objective will be attainable – but demanding. An objective which demands too much (e.g. work to be completed in too short a span of time) is a recipe for disaster. Even if it is not obvious at the start, the time will come when those responsible for achieving the objective will realise that it is not attainable. At this point morale and confidence will fall rapidly. It will then be necessary to lower the sights of both management and the implementers, and this in itself can cause friction between them and frustration all round. There is then a tendency for the whole scheme to 'go sour'.

However, too low a target may mean that the best may not be gained from the situation, opportunities may be lost or the problem dealt with less effectively than might otherwise be the case. The objective should be sufficiently demanding to pose a challenge and be designed to get the best possible (i.e. practicable) result.

3. The objective should be clear and understandable. Sometimes the more pompous type of senior executive will draft an objective more as a personal public relations exercise than as a sound work-a-day statement of what is to be done. Elaborate and often meaningless expressions should be avoided.

   Here are some examples from real-life documents:
   - '. . . a combination of factors comprised is our picture of success . . .'
   - '. . . adopt a holistic stance in determination of corporate development plans . . .'
   - '. . . maximisation of company and individual attainment is a fundamental basis upon which the new arrangements are predicated'.

   This kind of rubbish may delight its author, but will do nothing to clarify what is actually wanted. Whatever words and expressions are used in the objective, they should be understandable to everyone from shop-floor to boardroom. Clarity is improved by brevity and it is likely that any objective drafted in more than about fifty words could be improved.

4. The objective must be consistent with any objectives set elsewhere in the organisation and supportive of those objectives. This requirement can be extended to include compatibility with existing working methods and standards of performance. There is not much to be gained by solving a problem in one area but creating another somewhere else at the same time.

5. Performance against the objective must be measurable in some way. Ideally, this will be in clear numerical terms such as costs, income, speeds, volumes and the like.

## The next step – constructing a plan of action

A good plan of action will restate the objective, to make sure no one loses sight of it, and will include the following minimum points:

- a clear statement of who is in overall charge;
- a timetable of action steps;
- who is responsible for each action;
- how progress will be monitored;
- budgets and cash-flow.

The action steps can include a wide variety of possibilities and, taking the example of a computer system, will cover:

system design
programming or software purchase
hardware acquisition
hardware installation
space allocation
staff training
testing schedules and design of test data
de-bugging and post-implementation support.

The timetable for such a series of actions must be clearly set out and the simplified network system illustrated in Figure 3.18 on page 116 is a good way to do it.

In cases where the project is large and involves several people, checklists of actions (and required completion dates) should be provided to all the individuals involved. This means that each person has a clear understanding of his or her part in the plan.

For example, suppose that Mrs Jones is to be responsible for staff training. Her checklist could look something like the example shown in Figure 5.1.

Armed with this checklist Mrs Jones will be able to carry out her task knowing exactly what is expected of her. If, for any reason, Mrs Jones fails to achieve a target date – or, preferably, realises in advance that this is likely – she can advise the project leader who can then take appropriate action. Should Mrs Jones fall behind schedule (or get ahead of it), this is likely to have an effect on work to be done by other people. The project leader will have the option of rescheduling work to limit damage or gain an advantage and possibly issue revised checklists. At all events the checklists provide a mechanism for controlling activities.

| STAFF TRAINING CHECKLIST – MRS JONES | | |
|---|---|---|
| **Action to be taken** | **Deadline date** | **Remarks** |
| **1.** Interview all department heads to ascertain list of trainees | 10 Nov. | Ensure expected new recruits are included |
| **2.** Confirm list of subjects to be learned by each trainee | 15 Nov. | Liaise with systems analyst |
| **3.** Prepare training material | 30 Nov. | Obtain sample listings from programmer |
| **4.** Organise training room with appropriate number of terminals | 15 Dec. | Check cabling position with electrician and monitor installation |
| **5.** Prepare training schedule and advise department heads and trainees | 20 Dec. | |

*Figure 5.1* Staff training checklist

## *Who is really in charge?*

The plan should state who is responsible for running the show and making sure that objectives are achieved. This requirement is not met simply by naming the person responsible. Whoever is held responsible must have not only the necessary financial and other resources, but also the 'clout' required to get things done. An appropriate and high degree of delegated authority is needed so that the project leader can get on with the job, and make financial and other decisions as things go along. By all means set parameters (hopefully fairly wide), but never put the responsible person in a position where he or she must ask for routine decisions to be made by his or her boss or bosses. This is the classic recipe for delay.

Chief executives and other VIPs who insist on having everything referred to them are a menace. They are not likely to be aware of the detail of what is happening and will either make the wrong decision or spend an eternity being educated about the facts before they feel able to pronounce.

The sensible chief executive will only insist on being consulted if matters of policy are involved, significant *new* factors have emerged, or his or her support is required to get something done.

## Manage by exception

VIPs can save time by only being informed if something is *not* going according to plan. Weekly or monthly reports which simply say that everything is going along as required waste the time of the VIPs and the time of the people doing the job.

A good policy is to instruct the project leader to report only if something is adrift *and to say what is being done to correct the situation*.

## Don't carve the plan on stone

If you carve your plan on tablets of stone you might as well erect it in your local graveyard because that is where your plan is likely to end up. Since no one can foresee what is going to happen in the future a degree of flexibility is required in *how* to reach the objective, even if the objective itself remains unchanged. This is another reason for delegating authority to the individual given the job of implementing the solution.

Particularly important is the inclusion of some contingency action. It is often the case – particularly in planning in respect to a complex problem – that you will be able to anticipate results which may vary from what is hoped for or expected. For instance:

- machine speeds may not reach the manufacturer's claims;
- sales may be less than (or greater than) expected;
- costs may rise unexpectedly;
- a customer may cancel a large order;
- a key employee may resign or go sick;

- some aspects of the plan may take longer to carry through than was estimated, or some aspects may turn out to be easier and completed more quickly.

A good plan will make allowances for the possibility of some of these alternatives happening and a sub-plan of contingency action will be included. It is highly desirable, before implementation takes place, to identify perhaps four or five of the *key* results and to prepare a course of alternative action *in advance*. Should it become necessary the contingency action can be kicked off immediately it is indicated. This avoids the frustrating experience of having to call a halt to proceedings while an agonising rethink is undertaken.

### *Is your plan a good one?*

Your plan, like your objective, should satisfy a number of criteria. Here is a checklist to test the quality of your plan.

- Does the plan include a timetable of action steps?
- Are the people responsible for carrying out the plan (or its parts) named?
- Has adequate provision been made for all the resources required – human, financial, material?
- Have contingency actions been included?
- Does the plan force both groups and individuals to work systematically?
- Is sufficient flexibility built in?
- Is decision-making delegated to the 'action level'?

## The implementation cycle

Implementation is an important process within the problem-solving process and it will follow a cycle of events with flexibility built in. This cycle is illustrated in Figure 5.2.

We will now follow the cycle through and examine what is required at each stage.

Assume that the objective has been well defined in terms which mean something and that the plan has been put together.

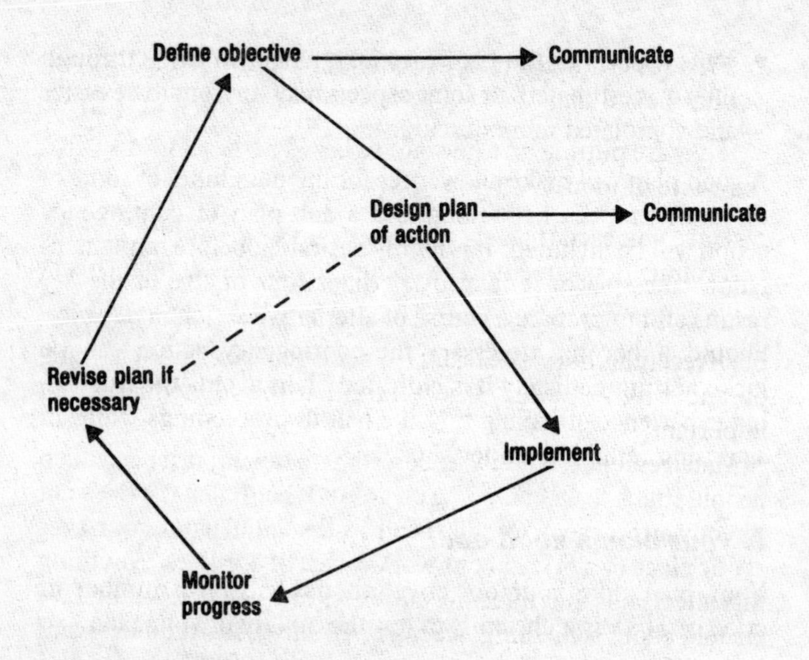


*Figure* 5.2 The cycle of implementation

As will be seen in Figure 5.2 communication is necessary before implementation can proceed.

## Communicating the objective and the plan

Good communication is a fundamental requirement for the success of your plan. If people do not know what you want to do *and why*, full co-operation becomes virtually impossible. Your plan may be simple and involve only a few people, in which case you may feel that only limited communication is needed. You may be right – but you should still think about it!

Look back at your own experiences and how you and your colleagues have reacted to discovering (informally) that a change is being made. Even the most trivial change, if not explained, can give rise to anything from cynicism to outright anger. Have you ever heard expressions such as these?

> 'They are moving the post room again. They must want something to do.'

'Fred says we are getting a new telex machine. What's wrong with the old one?'

'They are putting up a new notice board in the canteen. What a waste of money.'

'Have you seen the new expense claim form? A pity that the accounts department have nothing better to do than dream up new forms.'

Such reactions normally result from not being told what is going on and why – leading to a feeling that the individual is not important.

Management can easily underestimate the importance which people attach to what is going on around them even if it does not directly affect them. We all spend a substantial part of our lives at our place of work and our work is part of our lives. Anything that affects it is thus affecting our lives. The paradox is that if we *are* told about something, we may well shrug our shoulders and be indifferent to it, but if we are *not* told we feel offended and tend to oppose the change when it becomes apparent.

The golden rule therefore is 'If in doubt – tell them'.

**What should we tell them?**

In addition to what is going to happen and why, people like to know the following:

- who will be doing the job;
- when the work will be done;
- who will be affected.

The people directly affected will need to know *how* they will be affected, e.g.:

- any training or retraining they will receive;
- how their work will change.

They may also need reassurance if the changes are likely to give rise to fears of redundancy, loss of status, reduced earnings or any other adverse aspects. If you don't tell them then rumours will develop and you can bet that the rumour will include all the bad things.

**Another effect of rumours**

The optimists will assume that they will do well out of the scheme and the pessimists that they will do badly. The chances are that the optimists will end up disappointed and the pessimists confirmed in their worst fears. At all events morale will take a dive.

**What else will happen if we don't tell them?**

The obvious answer is that co-operation will be limited. Not only is there a natural reaction to be unwilling to co-operate, but if people are not aware of what you want from them then there is no way that they *can* be expected to co-operate.

**How should we tell them?**

There are a number of ways in which a company can communicate with its employees – or, to state it more accurately, can *try* to communicate.

The worst method is a piece of paper stuck on a notice board. Do you know where your notice board is? And if you do, when did you last look at it?

Some companies make a real effort to put their notice boards in prominent places and try to make them attractive. Sadly, many do not, with the result that the notice board is:

- hidden away in a dark corner at the end of the passageway leading to the basement;
- covered in out-of-date notices;
- a place where employees pin up cartoons and other items culled from the press – often with added comments.

One company had such a notice board on which there was a photocopy of a page from a magazine. The magazine article was in praise of the company and management thought that the staff would find it inspiring. The article included a photograph of the chairman whose smiling face was embellished with the usual moustache by a passing employee. Someone else added devil's horns. This item remained on the board for some months – which showed how little attention was paid to the board by management.

**What about a memo?**

The memorandum circulated to employees is a better method of communicating, at least in so far as each employee can have his or her own copy. This makes the message more personal and increases the chance that employees will read it.

However, memoranda cannot answer questions and are prone to a style of management-speak which is often obscure and sometimes pompous. The fact is that the written word has no tone of voice.

**The best method**

Nothing beats face-to-face briefing sessions. These have impact and enable participants to make comments and ask questions.

Briefing sessions do, of course, take up valuable time and are more expensive to hold than notices or memoranda. The expense is normally worth it and is usually far less than the cost of a mess caused by a failure properly to get the message across. In addition, the comments and questions asked can provide very valuable feedback and may reveal weaknesses in the plan which can be corrected before going any further. However, beware of the hierarchical briefing session system. This is the arrangement where the big boss tells the medium bosses who tell the little bosses who tell the troops.

In particular, avoid briefing employees via shop stewards or other so-called employee representatives. They will give the people *their interpretation* of the message and will, in effect, be controlling the project.

In *The Renewal Factor* by Robert H. Waterman (Bantam Press), the chairman of Cummins Engine (USA) is quoted as saying 'By the time the message gets passed down from the person who attended the staff meeting to the people who need to know it is so diluted and different it is worthless'. This sums the issue up nicely.

The method adopted by Cummins involves the managing director recording tapes of what he wants to communicate. These are made available to employees and are followed by face-to-face briefing sessions with groups of about fifty employees at a time. This method deals with the oft-mentioned problem that there are too many people around for everyone to be told personally and face-to-face. In addition, a good chief executive will want to see and hear his or her employees, and to be seen and heard by them. Briefing sessions provide an ideal opportunity.

### *Moving ahead*

Once the initial communication is complete, the plan can be put into action. This does not mean that all communication is now finished with as the plan itself should include continued communication both to keep people informed on progress and to co-ordinate activities. Co-ordination and control of the work will require a formal feedback system.

## Monitoring progress

A good monitoring system will achieve four things:

- accurate and usable information to enable management to assess progress against the plan and the objectives;
- assistance in predicting future events and progress;
- help in diagnosing the causes of any obstacles encountered;
- indication of whether either plan, objective or both require revision.

None of these requirements is likely to be met unless a formal monitoring system is set up. It is not enough just to say that everyone has his or her checklist and knows what to do. Nor is it enough to say 'We will have to get-together every now and then to see how things are going.'

In order to meet the four characteristics of a good monitoring system, methods must be found to ensure the following.

1. Feedback is sufficiently comprehensive to enable an accurate assessment of progress to be made. All aspects must be covered by the monitoring system and the emphasis must be *balanced*. This means avoiding concentrating over much on one or two aspects such as sales levels or cash-flow.

   The less exciting aspects require equal attention. A

subject which is frequently given too little attention in a major scheme is training – which is often dumped on the shoulders of a junior and poorly briefed training officer and then virtually ignored.

Another topic that is often neglected is the administration side. A plan which came unstuck involved setting up a branch office some two hundred miles from base. Communications were vital but the arrangements for installing telephones and fax were left to a junior assistant – who had little experience and limited authority. No monitoring of progress was arranged and delays in getting the telephone company to install its equipment were not noticed until it was too late. All the effort had been concentrated on sales activities and liaison with customers.

2. Feedback must be timely. Any significant events or developing trends must be reported in time for effective action to be taken. We are all familiar with plaintive cries such as, 'I wish I had known that last week . . .' or 'Why was I not told about this before we . . .'

   A positive arrangement may be needed to report back key information on a regular basis. There may be some information which should be listed as requiring communication on an immediate 'real-time' basis.

3. Feedback must be precise in some cases. The degree of precision required for reporting back should be considered and agreed. Reporting by exception can be used to save time and effort, as can approximations, if these are enough to maintain control. Care is needed, however, to identify cases where absolute precision is essential.

## *Choosing the monitoring methods*

There are a number of basic alternative methods to choose from. Whichever are chosen must obviously be appropriate to the situation, but they should:

- be as few as possible;
- be as simple as possible;

- result in information which can be acted upon, i.e. not just history of academic interest only;
- provide data which are capable of being compared with some 'benchmark' such as times, dates, volumes and costs;
- provide data which help to forecast future events and trends;
- assist in co-ordinating activities where several people are involved in different parts of the implementation plan.

## Some ways and means

### Team briefing and de-briefing sessions

If two or more people are responsible for aspects of implementation they *need to meet* at regular intervals. It is not enough to agree to meet 'when there is something to discuss' as, praiseworthy though this idea may be as a means to avoid wasting time, it rarely works well. In particular, things start to go wrong when one or other of the team members cannot get to an ad hoc meeting. In addition it is often the case that something that one team member thinks is not worth discussing may be of great significance to another member who would very much like to hear about it.

A regular meeting of the team members should be built into the implementation plan. If, say, Friday afternoons are fixed for a meeting then team members can arrange their personal timetable accordingly.

Regular meetings can have a basic agenda of regular items to be covered. These could include:

- briefing by the team leader, e.g. on any policy or other changes;
- review of progress against the timetable;
- difficulties encountered and the action taken;
- any problem areas for which one team member would like to have the advice of other members.

The last item can be particularly helpful and avoids an uncomfortable feeling of isolation when a team member is struggling along, perhaps geographically cut off from colleagues.

Whatever the agenda may be, good chairmanship is essential. It is all too easy for team sessions to deteriorate into cosy and inconsequential chit-chat about everything and anything.

One way to get the best out of the meeting is for the chairperson, having completed any briefing of the team as a whole, to go round the group one at a time. Each person is asked to say anything he or she has to say under each agenda item – and if there is nothing to say they should simply say so.

One successful manager holds his meetings with all the participants standing up. This virtually eliminates any unnecessary talking and normally results in all the essentials being covered in ten minutes or so.

**Visual aids**

A large chart on which progress is recorded (e.g. lists of jobs against dates with completion ticked) will often enable progress – or lack of it – to be seen at a glance.

The clear visual record has the advantages that:

- it is a constant nagging reminder;
- everyone can see it and know what is going on.

The chart can be updated by individual team members who mark completion dates or whatever against their own part of the job. The team leader can then see who has done what and be in a position to offer support to anyone who is lagging behind before a situation becomes critical.

**Pieces of paper**

Some managers are fond of weekly or monthly reports. These are often a time-consuming nonsense and as far as possible should be replaced with something else.

If you *must* have reports, at least make sure that everyone reports in the same format against standard headings. This will make assimilation of the information easier and will discourage rambling essays.

Information can often be fed back using documents which have already been prepared – or copies of them.

For example, a copy of a sales order or a delivery note can be used to communicate that a transaction has taken place without having to write a memo saying so.

### *Monitor to motivate*

A good monitoring system in which achievement against the programme of work is available for all to see can have a motivating effect. Seeing the results emerging is at least satisfying and when the people involved can see that a target will be reached with a little more effort, that effort is almost always forthcoming.

However, it is often argued that the effect of seeing that work is *not* going according to plan is demotivating and for this reason failure should not be publicised! In fact, this thinking is way off target. First of all, any hiccups should not be hidden away or nothing will be done to put things right. Second, a degree of adversity can result in a well-led team banding together even more closely with an enhanced determination to achieve the right results.

## Revising the plan – or the objective

In Figure 5.2 monitoring progress is followed in the cycle of events by revision of either the plan or the objective – or both.

Revision may not be necessary if the expectations on which the plan was based, or the chosen solution to the problem, turn out to have been correct. However, remember the famous Murphy's law which states that 'If there is anything which can go wrong it will go wrong'.

In real life even the best plans need adjusting from time to time, sometimes to the extent of bringing in the contingency plans which should have been worked out at the outset. Minor adjustments can normally be taken in the stride of the implementation team, but anything significant should be thought through as carefully as the original plan. Questions such as these should be asked formally:

- How does this change (or whatever) affect timing?

- Will more (or less) cash or other resources be needed?
- How will this affect other company objectives, methods, departments?
- Will solution of the problem now be easier or more difficult and what longer-term effects will result?
- Who needs to be informed?

The consequences of changing direction require careful evaluation – if only to guide your thinking into the best way to bring about the change.

At all events, if a need to change direction becomes apparent don't hesitate to do it. Clinging on to the old plan for reasons of pride, politics or whatever will create new problems and you could find yourself back at square one.

# SOURCES OF FURTHER INFORMATION

## Statistics

Described as a primer for non-mathematicians, *Statistics Without Tears* by Derek Rowntree (Pelican) is a useful book for those wishing to delve further into statistical method.

The book covers sampling in some detail and deals with making estimates and inferences. The last chapter deals with the analysis of mathematical relationships, e.g. correlation.

*How To Lie With Statistics* by Darrell Huff (Pelican) is a very readable book. The author shows how misusing data can result in misleading conclusions and emphasises the care needed if graphs and the like are to be truly helpful.

## Operational research

*Operational Research* by P. Harrison (Mitchell Beazley) covers the basic mathematics of linear programming and other techniques. This book will be of interest to anyone who is not content to allow computer software to do the work without understanding what lies behind it.

## Financial decision-making

The evaluation of business strategies from a financial point of view is covered in *Financial Decision Making* by Brian Pizzala (Mercury). Particularly helpful is the advice he gives on pricing strategies – including a pricing model.

## Ideas and innovation

*Managing for Innovation* by N. Smith and M. Ainsworth (Mercury) deals with removing barriers to innovation and how to use ideas to maximum effect.

Strategies for implementing change are discussed in *Making Change Work* by Edgar Wille and Philip Hodgson (Mercury). This book also deals with the important subject of how to overcome resistance to change in others.

# INDEX

## Piatkus Business Books

Piatkus Business Books have been created for people like you, busy executives and managers who need expert knowledge readily available in a clear and easy-to-follow format. All the books are written by specialists in their field. They will help you improve your skills quickly and effortlessly in the workplace and on a personal level.

Each book is packed with ideas and good advice which can be put into practice immediately. Titles include:

*General Management Skills*

**Brain Power: The 12-Week Mental Training Programme** Marilyn vos Savant and Leonore Fleischer
**The Complete Time Management System** Christian H. Godefroy and John Clark
**Confident Decision Making** J. Edward Russo and Paul J. H. Schoemaker
**Dealing with Difficult People** Roberta Cava
**The Energy Factor: How to Motivate Your Workforce** Art McNeil
**Firing on All Cylinders: Tried and Tested Techniques to Improve the Performance of Your Organisation** Jim Clemmer with Barry Sheehy
**How to Be Your Own PR Expert: The Complete Guide to Publicity and Public Relations** Bill Penn
**How to Develop and Profit from Your Creative Powers** Michael LeBoeuf
**The Influential Manager: How to Use Company Politics Constructively** Lee Bryce
**Leadership Skills for Every Manager** Jim Clemmer and Art McNeil
**Your Memory: How It Works and How to Improve It** Kenneth L. Higbee

*Sales and Customer Services*

**The Art of the Hard Sell** Robert L. Shook
**How to Close Every Sale** Joe Girard with Robert L. Shook
**How to Succeed in Network Marketing** Leonard S. Hawkins
**How to Win Customers and Keep Them for Life** Michael LeBoeuf
**Selling by Direct Mail** John W. Graham and Susan K. Jones
**Telephone Selling Techniques that Really Work** Bill Good

*Presentation and Communication*

**Better Business Writing** Maryann V. Piotrowski

**The Complete Book of Business Etiquette** Lynne Brennan and David Block

**Confident Conversation: How to Talk in any Business or Social Situation** Dr Lillian Glass

**Powerspeak: The Complete Guide to Public Speaking and Communication** Dorothy Leeds

**The PowerTalk System: How to Communicate Effectively** Christian H. Godefroy and Stephanie Barrat

**Personal Power: How to Achieve Influence and Success in Your Professional Life** Philippa Davies

**Your Total Image: How to Communicate Success** Philippa Davies

*Careers*

**The Influential Woman: How to Achieve Success Without Losing Your Femininity** Lee Bryce

**Marketing Yourself: How to Sell Yourself and Get the Jobs You've Always Wanted** Dorothy Leeds

**Networking and Mentoring: A Woman's Guide** Dr Lily Segerman-Peck

**The Perfect CV: How to Get the Job You Really Want** Tom Jackson

*Small Business*

**The Best Person for the Job: Where to Find Them and How to Keep Them** Malcolm Bird

**How to Collect the Money You Are Owed** Malcolm Bird

**Making Profits: A Six-Month Action Plan for the Small Business** Malcolm Bird

**Organise Yourself** Ronni Eisenberg with Kate Kelly

## MAKING PROFITS

by Malcolm Bird

In order to increase the profitability of your company you need to cut your costs and increase your revenue. *Making Profits* is packed with practical, proven techniques – short-term and long-term – that you can put into action today.

- Learn how to be your own management consultant
- Discover the fastest ways to get your money in
- Slash your overheads and administration costs
- Maximise your sales force
- Make your advertising and promotion more effective
- Plan now for future expansion and growth

*Making Profits* is a book that will pay dividends every time. No company executive or busy entrepreneur can afford to be without a copy.

Malcolm Bird is a management consultant and author of several business books.

## HOW TO WIN CUSTOMERS AND KEEP THEM FOR LIFE

by Michael LeBoeuf

*How to Win Customers and Keep Them for Life* will be the most important sales aid you will ever have. It will tell you:

- How to provide the best quality customer service
- The reasons which make customers buy and come back
- How to be the kind of person customers like to buy from
- How to find more customers
- How to make customers recognise the fine service you give them
- The five best ways to keep customers coming back
- How to keep your customers happy

*How to Win Customers and Keep Them for Life* is a hard-hitting, action-ready, rewards and incentive programme for creating a winning sales team. Written by Michael LeBoeuf, one of America's foremost business consultants, this practical no-nonsense guide tells you everything you need to know about successful selling.

## CONFIDENT DECISION MAKING

by J. Edward Russo and Paul J. H. Schoemaker

This is the decision-making programme that executives have been waiting for. Buying this book could be among the best decisions you've ever made!

- Avoid the common decision traps of self-taught amateurs
- Learn how to 'frame' a problem correctly
- Recognise and make use of all relevant information
- Follow a scientific decision-making process
- Improve your management skills by making better and more confident decisions

J. Edward Russo is Associate Professor of Marketing and Behavioural Science at Cornell University's Johnson Graduate School of Management and Paul J. H. Schoemaker is Associate Professor of Decision Sciences and Policy in the Graduate School of Business at the University of Chicago.

## THE COMPLETE TIME MANAGEMENT SYSTEM

by Christian H. Godefroy and John Clark

*The Complete Time Management System* will change the way you work and think. It will increase your enjoyment of life and your chances of success. It will show you:

- How to do in 2 hours what you usually need 4 hours to do
- How to revive your concentration
- How to read 240 pages an hour
- How to make an important decision faster
- How to delegate
- How to organise your office
- How to shorten meetings
- And much, much more

Learn the secrets of time management and you will profit from them all your life.

Christian Godefroy is a training specialist, founder of a publishing company in France and best-selling author.

## HOW TO COLLECT THE MONEY YOU ARE OWED

by Malcolm Bird

Getting paid on time is vital for any business. In *How to Collect the Money You are Owed*, Malcolm Bird gives practical advice on how to organise your invoicing and money collecting systems, improve your cash flow and increase your profitability.

- Learn how to control your cash flow cycle
- Develop an efficient invoicing system
- Get to know your clients and how they operate
- Learn how to chase up money effectively
- Discover what to do if all else fails

*How to Collect the Money You are Owed* will help you save time and money. It is an essential handbook for every office.

Malcolm Bird is a management consultant and author of several business books.

## DEALING WITH DIFFICULT PEOPLE

by Roberta Cava

Whether you have to face angry or frustrated customers, or are troubled by irritating subordinates, manipulative bosses or non-communicative co-workers, *Dealing with Difficult People* contains proven strategies for handling stressful situations and defusing tensions calmly and professionally.

- Discover the main cause of customer frustration and anger – and how to alleviate it
- Learn ways to deal with specific problems and personality conflicts
- Find out how to increase your people skills and work better with others
- Reduce your own stress and anxiety and increase your confidence and enthusiasm for the job

Roberta Cava runs training and development seminars on interpersonal skills, assertiveness, time and stress management, personal and business development.